Integrating Microeconomic And Macroeconomic Price Systems

John P. Barrados, Ph.D. (Columbia)

TRAFFORD PUBLISHING

Order this book online at www.trafford.com
or email orders@trafford.com

Most Trafford titles are also available at major online book retailers.

Printed in Victoria, BC, Canada.

ISBN: 978-1-4251-0430-6 (sc)

*We at Trafford believe that it is the responsibility of us all, as both individuals
and corporations, to make choices that are environmentally and socially sound.
You, in turn, are supporting this responsible conduct each time you purchase a
Trafford book, or make use of our publishing services. To find out how you are
helping, please visit www.trafford.com/responsiblepublishing.html*

*Our mission is to efficiently provide the world's finest, most comprehensive
book publishing service, enabling every author to experience success.
To find out how to publish your book, your way, and have it available
worldwide, visit us online at www.trafford.com*

Trafford rev. 02/26/2010

 www.trafford.com

North America & international
toll-free: 1 888 232 4444 (USA & Canada)
phone: 250 383 6864 ♦ fax: 812 355 4082 ♦ email: info@trafford.com

Contents

Preface

Integrating Microeconomic And Macroeconomic Price Systems

We uncover in this book, an inconsistency in the general economic logic or rationale of orthodox price systems. This inconsistency arises because the systems lack a consistent general economic logic or rationale that extends across all of the systems.

Hence the systems lack an aspect to the behavior of individuals and firms that should ensure that the systems reflect this economic logic; and this restricts the generality of the systems.

However, we shall bring this aspect to the behavior of individuals and firms, and an associated aspect to rational behavior, into our new systems, to resolve the inconsistency in the orthodox systems. This leads to a more general approach to price systems compared to the orthodox approach.

There are many consequences of this new approach to price systems. However, we shall focus on a most general one. This is that this new approach integrates systems that are based on this approach.

This is in the sense that the systems based on our new approach, irrespective of the different forms of behavior of individual systems, are united or integrated by the general economic logic that stems from our new approach to price systems.

Consequently, our new approach to price systems integrates orthodox microeconomic and macroeconomic systems, systems which are dichotomized; and this integration will hence also be in terms of the systems' general economic logic or rationale.

We shall proceed by focusing on a specific system that represents our new systems, in order to show precisely how we integrate microeconomic and macroeconomic systems. This is a revised classical system which will be formed by our ridding the orthodox classical system of the inconsistency we uncover in orthodox price systems.

This revised classical system reflects a more general approach to microeconomics compared to the orthodox approach. This is because this revised classical system reflects the aspect to behavior, and associated rational behavior, that are missing from the orthodox systems.

Next, we shall show that our revised classical system, while being a long-run system, is not necessarily restricted to long-run states like the orthodox classical system. Hence the revised classical system can move to short-run states were behavior to change to short-run behavior.

That is, short-run or macroeconomic systems emerge from our revised classical system as behavior in the system changes to short-run behavior. Moreover, these short-run or macroeconomic systems will reflect the similar general logic that characterizes our revised classical system itself.

This reflects how we integrate microeconomic and macroeconomic systems from the perspective of microeconomic systems as represented by our revised classical system. Moreover, we shall draw on our new approach to price systems to show how the Keynesian macroeconomic system may, in principle, be given a satisfactory microeconomic character.

Hence our new approach to price systems provides a means to integrate microeconomic and macroeconomic systems from the perspective of both microeconomic and macroeconomic systems.

Consequently, our new approach to price systems, as reflected in our revised classical system, is more general than the orthodox approach. This is because this new approach ensures that all systems based on this approach are integrated.

This, to review, is in the sense that this approach brings into price systems, a common and consistent general economic logic. This unites the systems in terms of this general economic logic while allowing for the different forms of behavior of individual systems.

Whereas the orthodox approach to price systems does not bring such a common and consistent general economic logic into orthodox systems. This is because of the inconsistency we have uncovered that characterizes the orthodox approach to price systems.

This explains why orthodox price systems, such as microeconomic and macroeconomic systems, are dichotomized; since they lack the unifying general economic logic that characterizes our new systems.

This has been a very general description of the inconsistency we have uncovered in orthodox price systems; and we will have to put the general economic logic of price systems in a way that allows us to put our analysis into mathematical terms. This will be done in the following way.

All price systems are subject to limitation in resources hence the systems must reflect consistency with limitation in resources. That is, the quantities of goods demanded and the quantities supplied must each sum to a limited volume of resources underlying the systems.

Consequently, since all price systems must necessarily be consistent with limitation in resources, we may look on consistency with limitation in resources as reflecting the general economic logic that should extend across all price systems.

Next, we discussed how we shall bring into our new systems, an aspect to behavior that will bring the general logic of price systems into our new systems; and this aspect to behavior will capture consistency with limitation in resources in a manner that takes such consistency as a property of all of our new systems or of price systems in general.

This will account for the generality of our new approach to price systems. However, orthodox price systems lack the aspect to behavior we have described that characterizes our new systems; and this results in the orthodox systems being initially inconsistent in a mathematical sense.

Then the systems are made mathematically consistent; and this ensures that the systems are consistent with limitation in resources. However, while mathematical consistency ensures consistency of the orthodox systems with limitation in resources, this is ensured in a restricted manner.

This is because mathematical consistency ensures consistency of orthodox price systems with limitation in resources only as a property of each individual system rather than as a property that extends over all the systems.

Hence while each individual orthodox system is consistent with limitation in resources, the systems yet lack the general economic logic or rationale that extends across all price systems.

This is because this requires that consistency with limitation in resources be ensured in a manner that takes such consistency as a property of price systems in general. This, however, is not the case with orthodox systems; and this restricts the generality of the systems.

Chapter 1

The General Nature Of The Inconsistency In The Orthodox Classical System

1.1 Introduction

This chapter describes in a general way the inconsistency we have uncovered in the orthodox form of the classical system; and as well, we shall discuss how Keynes, in not uncovering this inconsistency, approached the classical system in a restricted manner.

We shall represent the orthodox classical system by a mathematical form of the system that was developed in neoclassical analysis. This system, which we refer to as Model A, while being developed in neoclassical analysis, is also widely taken as a formal version of the classical system.

Hence while we may refer to Model A as both classical and neoclassical, we shall find it convenient to refer to it as a classical system. Nonetheless, there are digressions in parts of the book on Model A when taken specifically as a neoclassical system.

Keynes held that the classical system is restricted in generality in being restricted to long-run states; and we shall find that Model A is indeed restricted in this way. However, we shall show that this is because of the inconsistency we uncover in the system.

Hence in resolving this inconsistency, we shall arrive at a form of the classical system that is not restricted to long-run states. This system, referred to as Model B, provides the basis for an approach to price systems that is more general than both the orthodox microeconomic and macroeconomic approaches to the systems.

This is reflected in this new approach providing the basis to integrate microeconomic and macroeconomic systems, systems that are dichotomized in the literature.

1.2 An Overview Of The Inconsistency In The Orthodox Classical System

There are two basic facets to price systems. First, there is a general logic to the systems that extends across all of the systems; and we shall take this general logic of price systems to be reflected in the systems being consistent with limitation in resources.

Consistency with limitation in resources is reflected in the quantities of goods demanded and supplied in price systems each summing to a limited volume of resources underlying the systems. Second, there is a specific form of behavior that characterizes individual systems.

Now the classical economists formulated a long-run system; and neoclassical economists systematized this classical system through a mathematical system, Model A. However, inconsistency arose when this was done. Let us discuss this inconsistency in a general way although we shall provide a more detailed analysis of this inconsistency in the following chapter.

We shall take consistency with limitation in resources as a general condition or requirement for consistency of price systems. Clearly, also, consistency with limited resources applies not only to individual systems but also applies across all price systems.

Hence behavior in price systems must be behavior that ensures consistency of the systems with limitation in resources irrespective of the differing forms of behavior of individual systems. Put another way, behavior in price systems must be behavior that ensures consistency of the systems with limited resources as a property of price systems in general.

However, Model A lacks this behavior; since we shall find that consistency with limitation in resources is ensured in the system as a property of this specific system. This is a reflection of the inconsistency we have uncovered in the system.

Moreover, this inconsistency also characterizes all systems based on the orthodox or neoclassical-type demand and supply functions such as characterize Model A. Hence it stems from the orthodox approach to price systems.

As a result, in resolving the inconsistency in Model A, we shall not only revise this specific system to give it a more general character. We shall also come upon a more general approach to price systems compared to the orthodox approach.

This is because we shall form systems that not only reflect the different forms of behavior of individual systems. These new systems will also reflect behavior that extends across all of the systems; and this behavior will capture consistency with limitation in resources as a property of all of the systems or of price systems in general.

This results in consistency with limitation in resources, or consistency of the general economic logic of our new systems, becoming a unifying element in the systems; and this provides the basis to integrate microeconomic and macroeconomic systems.

Whereas consistency with limitation in resources is captured in orthodox systems such as Model A as a property of each individual system. Hence the orthodox systems lose consistency with limitation in resources as a unifying element in the systems. This results in orthodox microeconomic and macroeconomic systems being dichotomized.

1.3 Further Remarks On The Inconsistency Of The Orthodox Classical System

Underlying all price systems are, first, a general economic logic that extends across all of the systems. This general economic logic is reflected in all systems being consistent with limitation in resources. Hence it should be captured in the systems as a property of all price systems or price systems in general. Second, there is a logic that is specific to each individual system.

However, orthodox price systems such as Model A are made consistent by being made mathematically consistent, and this ensures that Model A is consistent with limitation in resources. But this results in consistency with limitation in resources, which should apply across all price systems, being transformed into a logic that is specific to Model A.

This is because consistency with limited resources is ensured in Model A as a consequence of the system being made mathematically consistent.

We shall find, however, that the general economic logic that applies across all price systems, as reflected in consistency of the systems with limited resources, has to be captured through the general form of the systems' demand and supply functions; and we shall find that Model B's functions will reflect this general form.

As a result, Model B's functions will capture how consistency with limited resources is a property of price systems in general. As well, the functions will ensure that the specific

Model B is consistent with limitation in resources; and this will ensure that Model B is consistent in a mathematical sense.

Hence mathematical consistency of Model B will be a consequence of the general economic logic or rationale that extends over all price systems. Model A, however, is not based on the type of functions that will characterize Model B. Hence Model A does not reflect the general economic logic that should characterize all price systems. This leads to the system being initially inconsistent in a mathematical sense.

Then Model A is made consistent by mathematical consistency being imposed on the system; and this ensures that the system is consistent with limitation in resources. This, however, brings inconsistency into the system; since the system should be made consistent with limitation in resources by the behavior or economic rationale that extends across all price systems.

Hence to resolve Model A's inconsistency, we should base the system on the type of demand and supply functions that will characterize Model B. These functions will impose on the latter system, the condition for general economic consistency we have discussed. This, to review, is that consistency with limited resources be ensured in a manner that takes it as a property of all price systems.

Moreover, the functions will ensure that Model B is consistent in a mathematical sense. Hence through Model B, we shall resolve Model A's economic inconsistency as well as how this inconsistency is reflected in Model A in mathematical terms.

1.4 Keynes' Approach To The Classical System

Keynes' basic criticism of the classical system is that the system is restricted by Say's Law to long-run, full-employment states. Say's Law is an identity between the aggregate demand and supply of commodities, an identity that we shall cover in detail later in the book.

However, we shall find that this restriction of the classical system to long-run states results from the inconsistency we have uncovered in the system. Moreover, this inconsistency characterizes not only Model A but also the overall orthodox method of forming price systems.

Hence we must rid the orthodox approach to price systems of this inconsistency to resolve the problem of Model A being restricted to long-run states. This is the approach followed in this book to the problem of the classical system being restricted to long-run states. That is, we shall take this problem as a problem of orthodox price systems in general and will resolve it as such.

Keynes, however, took the problem of the classical system being restricted to long-run states as a problem of the specific classical system; and this is reflected in Keynes approaching this problem through his own specific system, his macroeconomic system, which he opposed to the classical system.

This meant, however, that Keynes could not resolve the problem of the classical system being restricted to long-run states in a fully satisfactory manner; since this requires that we take this problem, and resolve it, as a problem of orthodox price systems in general.

Hence while Keynes' system, unlike the classical system, can describe short-run states, his system is dichotomized from the classical long-run system. Moreover, there is no satisfactory basis in microeconomics for the Keynesian system.

In contrast, we shall revise the classical system, Model A, through Model B by our basing the latter system on the general logic we have described. This is a logic that characterizes not only individual price systems but also price systems in general. This will lead to a more general approach to price systems compared to the orthodox approach.

This will be reflected in Model B being characterized by a more general approach to microeconomics compared to the orthodox approach. As well, we shall find that Model B can move to short-run states were behavior to change.

Hence short-run or macroeconomic systems emerge from our revised classical system. This reflects how through our new approach to price systems, we shall integrate microeconomic and macroeconomic systems. Whereas, as we discussed, the classical microeconomic system and the Keynesian macroeconomic system are dichotomized.

1.5 The Restricted Microeconomic Character Of The Keynesian System

In order to resolve the problem of the classical system, Model A, being restricted to long-run states, we must rid the system of an incorrect form of Say's Law that characterizes the system. This is because it is this incorrect form of the Law that restricts Model A to long-run states.

Moreover, we shall find that the Keynesian system and Model B are both rid of this incorrect form of the Law. However, Keynes rid his system of Model A's Say's Law through macroeconomic analysis.

This is through Keynes allowing aggregate demand and supply of commodities to diverge in his system. Then aggregate demand and supply, in coming to equilibrium, determine overall output or income in the Keynesian system. This approach does give the Keynesian system a macroeconomic character.

However, it suppresses or abstracts from the microeconomics of the real part of the Keynesian system. This is because Keynes' overall output or income variable, and associated aggregate demand and supply functions, suppress the individual quantities of commodities and hence the commodity relative prices in the Keynesian system.

Hence the macroeconomic character of the Keynesian system comes at the expense of the microeconomics of the real part of the system. Let us now consider Model B.

This system is also rid of Model A's incorrect form of Say's Law which means that Model B, like the Keynesian system, is not restricted to long-run states. However, this is accomplished in Model B through microeconomic analysis.

This is because it is through microeconomic analysis that we shall rid Model B of the inconsistency we uncover in Model A; and this accounts for Model B being rid of Model A's incorrect form of Say's Law.

Consequently, while Model B has a macroeconomic character in not being restricted to long-run states, the system is yet a wholly microeconomic system. On the other hand, while the Keynesian system also has a macroeconomic character in not being restricted to long-run states, the microeconomics of the real part of the system is suppressed.

1.6 Why Keynes Did Not Uncover The Inconsistency In The Classical System

Keynes, in Chapters 2 and 3 of his *General Theory,* discussed how Say's Law restricts the classical system to long-run states.[1] Keynes, in these chapters, imputed an identity form of the Law to the classical system. That is, a form of the Law that takes the

---

[1] J.M.Keynes, *The General Theory Of Employment, Interest And Money* (New York, 1936), Chs. 2 and 3.

aggregate demand for commodities to be identical to the aggregate supply.[2]

This meant, to paraphrase Keynes, that if individuals and firms do not spend their resources on certain goods, they will spend them on other goods. This, in turn, given the classical assumption of perfect flexibility of prices, will keep the system in a long-run, full-employment state.

Should we focus on Say's Law as Keynes did in Chapters 2 and 3 of his *General Theory,* that is, apart from an explicit mathematical price system, we would always agree with Keynes that the classical system is restricted to long-run states by Say's Law.

Moreover, if we do shift to an explicit mathematical form of the classical system such as Model A, we find that this system confirms Keynes' view that the classical system is indeed restricted to long-run states by Say's Law.

What was required, however, was that we examine in detail the relationship between the economics and mathematics of Model A; and it was in so doing, that we uncovered an economic inconsistency in Model A that restricts the system to long-run states. There are several stages to our analysis:

First, Model A is initially inconsistent in a mathematical sense. Then Model A is made mathematically consistent by Say's Law being imposed on the system to eliminate a surplus equation.

Next, it will be shown that in making the system mathematically consistent, the system is made consistent with limitation in resources. This provided a clue that led us to uncover that there is an economic inconsistency in Model A and to ultimately resolve this inconsistency.

To review, Model A is made consistent with limitation in resources as a result of the system being made mathematically consistent. This, however, is an inconsistency. This is because consistency with limited resources is a condition for economic consistency of a system.

Hence it should be ensured by the behavior or economic rationale of the system; and in Chapter 2.3, we shall set out the aspect to the behavior of individuals and firms that ensures consistency of our new systems with limitation in resources.

However, Model A lacks this aspect to the behavior of individuals and firms; since, as discussed, the system is made consistent with limitation in resources as a result of the system

---

[2] On Say's Law see J.B. Say, *A Treatise on Political Economy,* trans. by C.R. Prinsep (1834), pps. 138-39. Say's Law will be discussed in more detail later in the book.

being made mathematically consistent by Say's Law; and this brings inconsistency into the system.

We shall, however, resolve this inconsistency through a new type of demand and supply functions that will form the basis for Model B, our revised classical system. These functions resolve the inconsistency of Model A; since the functions, and hence the behavior in Model B, ensures that the latter system is consistent with limitation in resources.

Moreover, we shall find that Model B, unlike Model A, is not restricted to long-run states. Hence Model B will move to short-run states were behavior to change to short-run behavior, the system hence having a macroeconomic character. Yet the system will be a microeconomic system in being based wholly on the behavior of the individual and the firm.

This revised classical system, we shall find, reflects an approach to price systems that is more general than both the orthodox microeconomic approach and Keynes' macroeconomic approach to the systems; and this new approach, as reflected in Model B, provides the basis to integrate microeconomic and macroeconomic systems.

1.7 Summary

This chapter first described in a general way the inconsistency we have uncovered in Model A, the orthodox form of the classical system. Clearly, all price systems are subject to limitation in resources. Hence behavior in the systems must be behavior that is consistent with limitation in resources.

Consistency with limited resources, to review, is reflected in the quantities of goods demanded and supplied each summing to a limited volume of resources underlying price systems; and we shall take consistency with limitation in resources as a general condition or requirement for consistency of all price systems.

Hence since all price systems are subject to limitation in resources, behavior in the systems should ensure consistency with limitation in all systems irrespective of the differing forms of behavior of individual systems.

This is behavior that captures consistency with limited resources as a property of all price systems. But Model A lacks this aspect to behavior; since consistency with limited resources is captured in this latter system as a property of this specific system. This is a reflection of the inconsistency we have uncovered in the system.

However, we shall resolve this inconsistency in Model A to come upon a revised form of the system, Model B. Moreover, this latter system is not, like Model A, restricted to long-run states. Instead, Model B can move to short-run states were behavior to change to short-run behavior.

Hence short-run or macroeconomic systems emerge from Model B, reflecting how this system integrates microeconomic and macroeconomic systems. Whereas the classical microeconomic system and the Keynesian macroeconomic system are dichotomized.

We also discussed how both Model B and the Keynesian system are rid of Model A's form of Say's Law that restricts the latter system to long-run states. Hence both Model B and the Keynesian system are not restricted to long-run states. This reflects how both systems have a macroeconomic character.

However, the microeconomics of the real part of the Keynesian system is suppressed whereas Model B is a wholly microeconomic system.

Chapter 2

Details Of The Inconsistency In Orthodox Price Systems

2.1 Introduction

We shall describe in detail in this chapter the inconsistency we have uncovered in orthodox microeconomic price systems. However, later in the book, we shall also discuss how this inconsistency also mars macroeconomic systems such as the Keynesian system.

We shall, to review, represent orthodox microeconomic price systems by a mathematical form of the orthodox classical system. This system, to be called Model A, was developed in neoclassical analysis but is also widely taken as a formal version of the classical system.

Hence while we may refer to Model A as both classical and neoclassical, we shall find it convenient to refer to it as a classical system. Nonetheless, there are digressions in parts of the book on Model A when the system is taken specifically as a neoclassical system.[3]

We shall also develop a revised form of Model A, to be called Model B, the latter system hence being a revised classical system. More generally, however, we shall look on Model A as reflecting the orthodox approach to microeconomic price systems and on Model B as reflecting our new approach to the systems.

We may base the new systems in the book precisely on the maximizing behavior of the individual and the firm. However, we shall simply take it that this maximizing behavior operates in the background of the systems rather than basing the systems in detail on this behavior. This allows us to focus on the core issue of the book.

This is reflected in our bringing into our new systems, an aspect to the behavior of individuals and firms, and an associated

---

[3] This system appears in many places in the literature being called at times a classical system and at other times a neoclassical system. See, for example, W.B.Hickman, "The Determinacy of Absolute Prices in Classical Economic Theory," *Econometrica*, 1950, where it is called a classical system. However, see Don Patinkin, *Money, Interest, And Prices* (2nd. ed., Harper and Row, New York, 1965), esp. Ch. VIII, where it is called a neoclassical system.

aspect to rational behavior, that are missing from the orthodox systems. Moreover, this is accomplished through our approaching the systems in the book as market systems, through focusing on the systems' market demand and supply relationships.

Finally, our focus in the book is on the general economic logic or rationale of price systems rather than on the different forms of behavior of individual systems; and we shall capture the general logic of our new systems through our revised classical system which is a long-run system.

However, we also need to consider short-run systems but we shall deal with such systems only by considering their general logic. Hence we do not deal with the specific forms of behavior that characterize short-run systems.

Nonetheless, the new approach to price systems set out in this book should be applied in detail to short-run systems. However, this is beyond the scope of the present book.

2.2 The Hidden Inconsistency In Orthodox Price Systems

Model A is based on demand and supply functions that stem from the maximizing behavior of the individual and the firm. However, the system is found to be initially inconsistent in a mathematical sense. Economists then proceed to make the system consistent by making it mathematically consistent; and mathematical consistency ensures consistency of the system's general logic.

This means that we can solve the system for its equilibrium quantities of commodities and its equilibrium prices. However, we must assume that Model A is subject to limited resources.

Hence mathematical consistency, in allowing us to solve for the system's equilibrium quantities and prices, also ensures that the quantities we solve for necessarily sum to the limited volume of resources underlying the system. As a result, mathematical consistency of Model A ensures that the system is consistent with limitation in resources.

This means that we are taking consistency with limitation in resources in price systems to mean that the quantities of commodities that individuals and firms demand and supply must each sum to the limited volume of resources of the systems.

Now we shall take consistency with limitation in resources as an overall condition or requirement for consistency of all price systems. Moreover, consistency with limitation in resources is an economic condition for consistency of price systems. This is because, as will be discussed in Section 2.3 below, it must be ensured by the behavior of individuals and firms.

Hence since we shall take consistency with limitation in resources to apply to all price systems, and since it is a condition for economic consistency of the systems, we shall take consistency with limited resources to reflect consistency of the systems' general economic logic.

We are now able to bring out how Model A, the orthodox classical system, is subject to an inconsistency.

As discussed, consistency with limited resources, or consistency of the general economic logic of a system, is an economic condition that must characterize the system. Hence it should be ensured by the behavior or economic rationale of the system.

Instead, as we have discussed, consistency with limitation in resources is ensured in Model A as a result of the system being made mathematically consistent. This is the inconsistency we have uncovered in Model A, an inconsistency that is economic in character; since it arises because an aspect to behavior is missing from the system.

This is the aspect to behavior that should ensure that the system is consistent with limitation in resources. Model A's demand and supply functions, however, lack this aspect to behavior, to explain why the system's functions do not ensure that the system is consistent with limitation in resources.

This causes the system to be initially inconsistent in a mathematical sense. Economists then impose mathematical consistency on the system; and this ensures that the system is consistent with limitation in resources.

As a result, mathematical consistency is given preference over economic consistency in ensuring that Model A is consistent with limitation in resources. Whereas the system should be made consistent with limitation in resources by the behavior or economic rationale of the system.

We shall, however, resolve Model A's economic inconsistency through Model B; since consistency of the latter system with limited resources, or consistency of the system's general economic logic, will be ensured by the system's behavior or economic rationale.

This is because it will be ensured by the system's demand and supply functions. That is, our new demand and supply functions of Model B will ensure that the quantities of commodities demanded and supplied each sum to the limited volume of resources underlying the system. There is now the issue of consistency of Model B's general logic.

This, of course, will be ensured as in orthodox price systems by Model B being made mathematically consistent. However, mathematical consistency enters Model B in quite a different way from how it enters Model A.

Mathematical consistency is imposed on Model A to make the system consistent; and this, as we discussed, gives mathematical consistency preference over economic consistency in ensuring consistency of the system with limited resources.

However, mathematical consistency in Model B will be a consequence of the system's general economic consistency, meaning consistency of the system with limitation in resources. This is because the system's demand and supply functions will automatically ensure that the system is consistent in a mathematical sense.

This resolves, through Model B, the mathematical reflection of Model A's economic inconsistency. This, to review, is reflected in mathematical consistency being given preference over economic consistency in ensuring consistency of Model A with limited resources.

Whereas mathematical consistency of Model B will be a consequence of the system's general economic consistency. Hence through Model B, we shall resolve Model A's economic inconsistency as well as how this inconsistency is reflected in Model A in mathematical terms.

We shall now set out the aspect to the behavior of individuals and firms that is missing from the orthodox price systems. This, to review, is the aspect to behavior that ensures that our new systems are consistent with limitation in resources.

Hence since consistency with limitation in resources applies across all of our new systems, we would expect that the aspect to behavior that ensures this also applies across all of our new systems; and we shall find that this is indeed the case.

2.3 The Aspect To Behavior That Is Missing From Orthodox Price Systems

We have discussed how the hidden inconsistency we have uncovered in orthodox price systems such as Model A is reflected in consistency with limited resources being ensured as a consequence of the systems being made mathematically consistent.

This is a mathematical reflection of what is an economic inconsistency in the systems. This is because it reflects how the demand and supply functions of the systems do not, in the first place, ensure that the systems are consistent with limitation in resources.

Then the mathematics of the systems is brought into the picture to ensure that the systems are consistent with limitation in resources. This happens as a consequence of the systems being made mathematically consistent. This means that an aspect to the behavior of individuals and firms is missing from the orthodox systems.

We may best bring out the nature of this aspect to behavior by running ahead to refer to a new type of demand and supply functions to be set out later in the book. These new functions will ensure that our new systems are consistent with limitation in resources. But what sort of behavior ensures this?

This is behavior that reflects how individuals and firms are aware that their resources are limited and hence they act in light of this awareness.

Clearly, this behavior is what causes our new type of demand and supply functions to ensure that our new systems are consistent with limitation in resources. This aspect to behavior, however, is missing from the orthodox-type functions.

This is because these latter functions do not ensure that the orthodox systems are consistent with limitation in resources. This results in mathematical consistency coming into the picture to ensure that the systems are consistent with limitation in resources, a mathematical reflection of the systems' economic inconsistency.

Finally, while we have now set out the new aspect to the behavior of individuals and firms that will characterize our new systems, we need to show how this behavior translates into a new aspect to rational behavior that will hence also characterize our new systems. This will be done in Chapter 6.9.

2.4 Comparing The New And The Orthodox-Type Demand And Supply Functions

Orthodox demand and supply functions are based on the maximizing behavior of the individual and the firm; and this behavior, which is implied in our new systems, must meet the well-known conditions or axioms for consistency and rationality of behavior set out in the literature.[4]

However, there is a more general condition for consistency and rationality of behavior that the orthodox functions do not meet. This is because the orthodox functions do not reflect how individuals and firms must be taken to be aware that their resources are limited and hence they act in light of this awareness.

As a result, the orthodox functions do not ensure that the orthodox systems are consistent with limitation in resources.

This is the underlying cause of the inconsistency in orthodox price systems uncovered in this book, an inconsistency that is clearly economic in character. Let us now consider our new type of demand and supply functions.

These new demand and supply functions are consistent with the maximizing behavior of individuals and firms although we shall leave this behavior implicit in our analysis.

However, unlike the orthodox-type functions, our new functions will also reflect how individuals and firms are aware that their resources are limited and hence they act in light of this awareness. As a result, the new functions will ensure that our new systems are consistent with limitation in resources.

Consequently, through these new systems, we shall resolve the inconsistency in orthodox price systems uncovered in this book; since, to review, this inconsistency arises because the orthodox-type functions do not ensure that the orthodox systems are consistent with limitation in resources.

2.5 How The Inconsistency In The Classical System Will Be Resolved

Clearly, the hidden inconsistency we have uncovered in Model A must be resolved in the following way. We must revise the system to ensure that consistency of the system's general economic logic, meaning consistency of the system with limited resources, is ensured by the system's behavior or economic rationale.

This means that we must write a new type of demand and supply functions that will reflect behavior that is consistent with limitation in resources. This, to review, is behavior reflected in

---

[4] On these conditions or axioms for consistency and rationality of behavior in price systems see, for example, J.M. Henderson and R.E. Quandt, *Microeconomic Theory: A Mathematical Approach* (New York, 1958), Chs. 2 and 3, and W.S. Vickrey, *Microstatics* (Harcourt, Brace and World, 1964), Chs. 2 and 4.

individuals and firms being taken to be aware that their resources are limited and hence they act in light of this awareness.

We shall form such functions that will be the basis for Model B, our revised form of Model A. Hence these new functions will ensure that Model B is consistent with limitation in resources. That is, Model B's functions will ensure that the quantities of commodities demanded and supplied each sum to the limited volume of resources underlying the systems.

This means that through Model B, we shall resolve Model A's economic inconsistency. Moreover, Model B's functions will automatically ensure that the system is consistent in a mathematical sense.

Hence mathematical consistency of Model B will be a consequence of the system's general economic consistency, rather than overriding this general economic consistency as in Model A. As a result, through Model B, we shall resolve Model A's economic inconsistency as well as how this inconsistency is reflected in Model A in mathematical terms.

2.6 The General Logic And The General Economic Logic Of Price Systems

We shall give economic meaning to the *general logic* of price systems through casting consistency of this general logic in terms of consistency of the systems with limitation in resources. That is, in terms of consistency of the systems' *general economic logic.*

Hence we shall avoid having to make the systems' general logic consistent in the orthodox manner. That is, we shall avoid having to make the systems' general logic consistent simply by making the systems mathematically consistent. This is an approach which brings the inconsistency we have uncovered into orthodox systems such as Model A.

Instead, we shall ensure consistency of the general logic of our new systems by ensuring consistency of the systems with limited resources through the systems' demand and supply functions and hence through the systems' economic rationale.

That is, in ensuring consistency of the systems' *general economic logic,* meaning consistency of the systems with limited resources through the systems' demand and supply functions, we shall also automatically ensure that the systems' *general logic* is consistent.

This will be reflected in our ensuring consistency of the systems with limited resources also ensuring that the systems are consistent in a mathematical sense.

Hence consistency of the general logic of our new systems, in being reflected in mathematical consistency of the systems, will be a consequence of consistency of the systems' general economic logic, meaning consistency of the systems with limited resources.

We have in this analysis distinguished between consistency of the general economic logic of our new systems and consistency of the general logic of the systems.

Consistency of the systems' general economic logic was then taken to reflect consistency of the systems with limited resources. While consistency of the systems' general logic was taken to reflect mathematical consistency of the systems.

However, consistency of our new systems' general economic logic, meaning consistency of the systems with limited resources, will ensure consistency of the systems' general logic, as reflected in mathematical consistency of the systems. Nonetheless, our distinguishing between consistency of our new systems' general logic, and consistency of the systems' general economic logic, is most useful.

This is because it assists us in showing that consistency of a system's general logic, as reflected in the system being mathematically consistent, is not of itself sufficient to satisfactorily ensure that the system is consistent.

What is required is that mathematical consistency, and hence consistency of the system's general logic, be ensured as a consequence of consistency of the system's general economic logic, meaning consistency of the system with limited resources.

This, we shall find, is the case with Model B, our revised classical system, and systems based on a similar approach; and this will account for these systems having a more general character than the orthodox systems.

2.7 The Orthodox Approach To Consistency Of Price Systems

Let us review the orthodox mathematical rules for consistency of price systems. These rules are centered around the need to ensure equality between the number of independent equations and the number of variables or unknowns of a system. There are various qualifications to these rules as economists have pointed out.[5]

---

[5] See, for example, Vickrey, *op.cit.,* pps. 121-22.

Most economists, however, simply take equality between the number of independent equations and unknowns of a system to mean that it is reasonable to assume that the system is consistent. This is in the sense that one and the same set of variables can simultaneously satisfy every equation of the system. Moreover, it is also usually assumed that only one such set of variables exists.

However, while all price systems must meet the equation-counting rule in order to be consistent, we shall find that this rule occupies quite a different place in our new systems compared to orthodox systems.

This is because while it is a requirement or condition to be met by all systems, meeting this condition in our new systems will be a consequence of the general economic consistency of the systems. Hence it is not a rule to be imposed on a system but should be ensured by the behavior or economic rationale of the system.

We shall find, however, that mathematical consistency of the orthodox classical system, Model A, is not a result of consistency of the system's general economic rationale. Instead, mathematical consistency is imposed on the system from the outside; and this brings the inconsistency we have uncovered into the system.

2.8 Why The Inconsistency In The Classical System Remained Hidden

Model A, as we have discussed, is subject to an economic inconsistency since the behavior in the system, and hence the system's demand and supply functions, do not ensure that the system is consistent with limitation in resources.

This, in turn, results in Model A being initially inconsistent in a mathematical sense. However, this mathematical inconsistency really reflects the system's economic inconsistency, as it were, masquerading as a mathematical inconsistency.

Economists then proceed to make the system mathematically consistent; and in ensuring mathematical consistency of the system, the system is taken to be consistent. Hence mathematics is misused in the system.

This is because the system's initial mathematical inconsistency is the result of an economic inconsistency. Hence making Model A mathematically consistent implies using mathematical consistency to resolve an economic inconsistency in the system, which is impossible.

Consequently, as would be expected, the system remained inconsistent in an economic sense. This economic inconsistency, however, remained hidden.

This is because it became reflected in Model A being initially inconsistent in a mathematical sense. Economists then proceed to make the system mathematically consistent, leading them to conclude that the system is consistent.

This meant that the whole issue of the general economic consistency of the system, as reflected in consistency of the system with limited resources, shifted into the background; since Model A seemed indeed to be consistent. However, Model A was deemed to be consistent solely on the basis of it being consistent in a mathematical sense rather than in an economic sense.

2.9 Summary

We described in detail in this chapter, the inconsistency we have uncovered in orthodox microeconomic price systems. These are systems we represent by Model A, the orthodox classical system.

To review, Model A is inconsistent in an economic sense because the system lacks an aspect to the behavior of individuals and firms. This is the aspect to behavior that ensures that a system is consistent with limited resources.

More precisely, as discussed in Section 2.3, it is the aspect to behavior reflected in individuals and firms having to be taken to be aware that their resources are limited and hence they act in light of this awareness.

As a result, since this aspect to behavior is missing from Model A, the system's functions do not ensure that the system is consistent with limitation in resources. This, in turn, causes the system to be initially inconsistent in a mathematical sense.

Economists then proceed to make the system mathematically consistent; and this ensures that the system is consistent with limitation in resources. However, the system remains inconsistent in an economic sense.

This is because the system's economic inconsistency can only be satisfactorily resolved by revising the system's functions to make them ensure that the system is consistent with limitation in resources.

This is the course followed in the book through Model B; since Model B's functions will ensure that the latter system is consistent with limitation in resources. That is, Model B's functions will ensure that the quantities of commodities demanded and supplied each sum to the limited volume of resources underlying the system. Hence through Model B, we shall resolve Model A's economic inconsistency.

Moreover, we shall find that Model B is automatically consistent in a mathematical sense. As a result, through Model B, we shall not only resolve Model A's economic inconsistency; as well, through Model B, we shall resolve how this inconsistency is reflected in Model A in mathematical terms.

Chapter 3

The Orthodox Form Of The Classical System

3.1 Introduction

We shall now formally set out Model A, the orthodox classical system. Next, we shall discuss how the system is initially inconsistent in a mathematical sense. Model A is then made mathematically consistent by Say's Law being imposed on the system to eliminate a surplus equation.

However, while generally being taken to be consistent, we shall find that Model A reflects the inconsistency we have described, an inconsistency we shall review in the chapter.

Finally, we shall provide some preliminary remarks on the integration of microeconomic and macroeconomic systems in the book and on the macroeconomic character of our new systems. These analyses will bring out properties of our new price systems that result from our resolving the inconsistency we have uncovered in the orthodox systems.

3.2 Orthodox General Price Systems

Orthodox microeconomic price systems such as Model A are based on demand and supply functions that stem from the maximizing behavior of individuals and firms.[6] Hence these functions are intended to reflect the economic behavior of individuals and firms.

This is in the sense that the functions show the quantities of goods demanded and supplied at various prices, assuming that all other influences on these demands and supplies are fixed.

Among the latter are the tastes and preferences of individuals and firms as well as their resources. Also, population and the state of technology are held fixed. There is next the question of consistency of the systems.

---

[6] On this system see, for example, Hickman, *op. cit.,* pps. 9-20 and Patinkin, *op. cit.*, Ch. VIII.

Behavior in the systems must, of course, meet the well-known axioms or conditions for consistency and rationality of behavior set out in the literature.[7]

Moreover, we also discussed how economists ensure consistency of the general logic of orthodox systems such as Model A by making the systems mathematically consistent; and they use an equation-counting rule to ensure such consistency. This is through equating the number of independent equations and unknowns in the systems.

Consistency, when ensured by a system meeting this equation-counting rule, implies that one and the same set of variables can simultaneously satisfy every equation in the system. There are various qualifications to this rule.

However, it was also discussed how most economists simply take equality of the number of independent equations and unknowns in a system to mean that it is reasonable to assume that the system is consistent.

We also pointed out that economists usually assume that there exists only one set of variables that simultaneously satisfies every equation of a system. With this as background, let us now focus on the orthodox classical system, Model A.

3.3 The Classical Long-Run System

Model A, which we use to represent the orthodox classical system is a long-run, stationary system where change is ruled out with all activities hence being carried out in a similar manner day after day. This leads to "static expectations" in the system.[8] That is, individuals and firms, given a milieu where change is absent, are assumed to expect that current prices will continue to rule in the future.

There are other characteristics of such long-run systems which economists have set out in detail.[9] Let us, however, proceed to set out Model A. This system, as we discussed earlier, was developed in neoclassical analysis but is also widely taken as a formal version of the classical system.

---

[7] On these axioms or conditions for consistency and rationality of behavior see, for example, Henderson and Quandt, *op. cit.*, Chs. 2 and 3. Also, Vickrey, *op. cit.*, where Ch. 2 considers the consumer and Ch. 4 considers the firm.

[8] On "static expectations" see, for example, O.Lange, *Price Flexibility And Employment* (Bloomington, 1945), pps. 1 and 22.

[9] See, for example, Vickrey, *op. cit.*, pps. 15-19.

Hence while we may refer to Model A as both classical and neoclassical, we shall find it convenient to refer to it as classical system. Model A is shown below:

Model A

1. $D_j \equiv F_j[z]$

2. $S_j \equiv G_j[z]$

3. $E_j[z] \models 0$

There are n commodities in the system plus money, which is assumed to be a neutral medium-of-exchange. The variables D_j and S_j denote the quantities of commodities demanded and supplied, respectively, $j=1,2,3,...,n$.

There are also n money prices implicit in the system. Next, we take the ratios of these money prices to determine $(n-1)$ price ratios or relative prices, which we shall denote by z. Expressions (1) and (2) are Model A's commodity demand and supply functions, respectively.

Functions (1) indicate that the quantities of commodities demanded, the D_j, depend on the relative prices, the z. While functions (2) indicate that the quantities of commodities supplied, the S_j, also depend on the z.

These demand and supply functions also depend on the tastes and preferences of individuals and firms and on their resources, as well as on the other variables referred to earlier. These, however, are all assumed to be fixed hence we have not shown them explicitly.

Equations (3) are the system's commodity excess-demand equations. They are derived from the commodity demand and supply functions. This is by taking the differences between the quantity demanded and supplied in each market across the system. These differences or excess demands, like the quantities demanded and supplied, hence also depend only on the relative prices, the z.

3.4 Rational Behavior In Model A

Rational behavior requires that the demands and supplies of commodities depend only on real variables as opposed to nominal money variables. Real price variables are relative prices which we derived by taking the ratios of the money prices.

This is why we followed the literature and made the quantities demanded and supplied depend only on the relative prices. There is, however, a question of why we did not make the quantities demanded and supplied depend on the money prices.

This was not done since the money prices are nominal money variables rather than real variables. This is because a proportionate change in all money prices, which is a change in the price level, will leave the real or relative prices unchanged.

Hence it is a nominal monetary change rather than a real change, since while money prices have changed, the real or relative prices have remained unchanged. Consequently, were behavior made to depend on the money prices, behavior would change in response to such a nominal monetary change.

This would reflect irrational behavior, or what is referred to as "money illusion," since the real or relative prices have not changed.[10] Accordingly, it was to rule out such irrational behavior that we followed the literature and made the quantities demanded and supplied in Model A depend only on the relative prices, the z, rather than on the money prices.

This is referred to as imposing an "homogeneity postulate" on the system.[11] Let us now consider consistency of the system following orthodox analysis.

There are expressions implicit in Model A reflecting the demand and supply of money flows. These are derived from the money prices and the quantities of commodities demanded and supplied. However, these expressions are dependent on the commodity equations hence they cannot be the basis for an equilibrium constraint on the system.

This means that since there are n commodities in Model A, there are n demand and n supply functions in each of (1) and (2). As a result, there are also n excess-demand equations in (3). Whereas the unknowns or variables to be determined are the relative prices, which are only $(n-1)$ number.

Hence the number of equations exceeds the number of unknowns which means that the system may be overdetermined and inconsistent. That is, there are too many restrictions in the form of equations, compared to variables, that are imposed on the system. Consequently, they cannot all be met simultaneously.

---

[10] On the orthodox concept of "money illusion" see, for example, Patinkin, *op. cit.*, pps. 174-76. Patinkin, however, has an alternative approach to money illusion, see his *Money, Interest, and Prices,* pps. 22-3.

[11] See Patinkin, *op.cit.,* pps. 174-76.

There is, however, a further element to be brought into Model A which will eliminate its surplus equation to ensure consistency of the system.

3.5 Say's Law

Model A is also characterized by Say's Law. This, to review, is an identity between the aggregate demand and supply of commodities.[12] Economists explain the rationale for this identity in various ways.

Some take it to reflect a classical principle that individuals and firms sell commodities only to buy other commodities. That is, commodities are exchanged only for other commodities. This means that the aggregate demand and supply of commodities are identical, leading to Say's Law.

Other economists take Say's Law as reflecting a classical assumption that individuals and firms will supply commodities only when they intend to immediately use the money they receive from the commodities they supply to demand other commodities.

This also implies that the aggregate demand for commodities (ad) is identical to the aggregate supply (as) of commodities. These aggregate demand and supply variables are derived by measuring the individual quantities of commodities demanded (supplied) in a common unit then summing these quantities.

We show Say's Law below using expression (4), this expression indicating how, according to the Law, the aggregate demand for commodities is identical to the aggregate supply:

4. $ad \equiv as$

Economists then use this identity to eliminate the surplus equation in Model A to ensure equality of the number of independent equations and unknowns in the system, to make the system consistent.

Yet the system is subject to the hidden economic inconsistency we have uncovered that was described in the preceding chapter. Let us review this inconsistency.

---

[12] On Say's Law see J.B. Say, *op. cit.,* pps. 138-39. The form of the Law we use is frequently referred to as "Say's Identity," a term introduced by G.S. Becker and W.J. Baumol in "The Classical Monetary Theory: The Outcome of the Discussion," *Economica,* XIX (1952), pps. 356-7.

3.6 Review Of The Hidden Inconsistency Of The Classical System

Model A is inconsistent in an economic sense because the system's functions do not ensure that the system is consistent with limitation in resources. This is because the system lacks the aspect to behavior that should ensure that the system is consistent with limitation in resources.

This, to review, is the aspect to behavior that reflects how individuals and firms must be taken to be aware that their resources are limited and hence they act in light of this awareness.

Model A's economic inconsistency, in turn, results in the system being initially inconsistent in a mathematical sense. Economists then proceed to ensure consistency of Model A by making the system mathematically consistent; and mathematical consistency ensures that the system is consistent with limitation in resources.

Model A, however, remains inconsistent in an economic sense; since its economic inconsistency can only be satisfactorily resolved by revising the system's functions to make them ensure that the system is consistent with limitation in resources.

This is the course followed in this book through Model B; since Model B's functions will ensure that the latter system is consistent with limitation in resources. This will resolve, through Model B, Model A's economic inconsistency.

Moreover, we shall find that Model B is automatically consistent in a mathematical sense. Hence through Model B, we shall resolve Model A's economic inconsistency as well as how this inconsistency is reflected in Model A in mathematical terms.

3.7 Further Remarks On The Inconsistency Of Model A

Model A's inconsistency stems from the system's demand and supply functions having a restricted character since, as we have discussed, the functions lack an aspect to the behavior of individuals and firms.

This, to review, is the aspect to behavior that should ensure that the system is consistent with limitation in resources. This, in turn, brings an incorrect form of Say's Law into the system; and this form of the Law results in the system being restricted to long-run states.

Hence what is required to resolve the problem of Model A being restricted to long-run states is that Model A's functions be given a more general character; and this is the course followed in this book through Model B. Let us provide a sketch of this analysis.

We have discussed how Model A is initially inconsistent in a mathematical sense. Then Say's Law is imposed on the system to eliminate a surplus equation to make the system mathematically consistent. This, however, reflects a misuse of mathematics. This is because Say's Law is a truism or identity. Hence it should not be given a substantive role in a system.

Yet it is given a substantive role, as an external constraint, in being used to make Model A mathematically consistent. This accounts for an incorrect form the Law entering Model A; and it is this form of the Law that restricts the system to long-run states.

Clearly, however, it is because Model A's functions do not ensure mathematical consistency of Model A that this incorrect form of the Law is brought into the system. Hence the restriction of Model to long-run states is due to the restricted generality of the system's demand and supply functions.

We shall proceed to resolve the problem of Model A being restricted to long-run states by first removing Say's Law from Model A. This will be accomplished by our taking the Law as a true identity. This, as will be discussed in Chapter 5.4, is through our collapsing the aggregate demand and supply variables in the Say's Law identity into a single variable, a variable that reflects the overall output or income of the system.

Consequently, the Law cannot now be used to ensure mathematical consistency of Model A. Hence we need to revise the system's functions to give them a more general character so that the new functions may ensure mathematical consistency of the system.

This will be accomplished by our transforming Model A's functions into a more general type of functions that will characterize Model B. Moreover, we shall find that Model B is automatically consistent in a mathematical sense.

Hence we do not have to impose the Say's Law identity on Model B to make the system mathematically consistent. This rids Model B of the incorrect form of Say's Law of Model A that restricts the latter system to long-run states. As a result, Model B will not be restricted in this way.

Accordingly, it is the new approach to behavior reflected in Model B's functions that rids the latter system of Model A's incorrect form of Say's Law; and this will resolve, through

27

Model B, the problem of Model A being restricted to long-run states.

As a result, it is through the microeconomic analysis of Model B that we resolve the problem of the classical system being restricted to long-run states since Model B is wholly microeconomic in character.

Whereas Keynes removed Model A's form of Say's Law from his system through macroeconomic analysis. This, however, as will be discussed later in the book, results in the microeconomics of the real part of the Keynesian system being suppressed.

3.8 Integrating Microeconomic And Macroeconomic Price Systems

Overall, the integration of microeconomic and macroeconomic systems in this book stems from our resolving the inconsistency we uncover in orthodox price systems. Then in resolving this inconsistency as it characterizes the orthodox classical system, Model A, we shall arrive at a revised classical system, namely, Model B.

Moreover, we shall find that this revised classical system is rid of an incorrect form of Say's Law that restricts the orthodox classical system, Model A, to long-run states. This, however, only makes our revised classical system consistent, in principle, with being able to move among alternative states.

What is also required is that Model B be characterized by a behaviorally-determined overall output or income variable. Hence were behavior to change, this will change overall output to cause the system to actually move to alternative states; and we shall find that our revised classical system, Model B, is characterized by such a variable.

However, we shall find that this variable in Model B has a broader meaning compared to the meaning given to it in orthodox macroeconomic systems such as the Keynesian system. We shall illustrate this by setting up a condition for internal consistency of a macroeconomic system.

This is that the way in which the system is made consistent, in principle, with being able to move to alternative states, must be consistent with the actual means where it is made to move to alternative states.

That is, it must be consistent with the nature of the system's behaviorally-determined overall output or income variable; and the Keynesian system and our revised classical system both meet this condition. Yet there is a significant difference between the systems. Let us first focus on the Keynesian system.

This system is rid of Model A's Say's Law that restricts the latter system to long-run states hence the Keynesian system is consistent, in principle, with being able to move to alternative states. However, Keynes rid his system of Model A's Say's Law through macroeconomic analysis; since Keynes removed this form of the Law from his system by allowing aggregate demand and supply of commodities to diverge.

Moreover, the Keynesian system's overall output or income variable is also macroeconomic in character; since it is an aggregative variable that suppresses the individual quantities of commodities in the real part of the Keynesian system.

This reflects how the Keynesian system meets our condition for internal consistency of a macroeconomic system. However, this is through macroeconomic analysis. Let us now consider our revised classical system, Model B.

We shall also rid this system of the incorrect form of Say's Law that restricts the orthodox classical system to long-run states. However, this is through microeconomic analysis.

This is because we shall resolve the inconsistency we uncover in the orthodox classical system, Model A, by revising, through Model B, the microeconomics of Model A; and this rids our revised classical system, Model B, of the Say's Law of Model A that restricts this latter system to long-run states. Hence Model B can move to alternative states as behavior changes.

Next, to meet our condition for internal consistency of a macroeconomic system, Model B must also be characterized by a behaviorally-determined overall output or income variable. Moreover, Model B's behaviorally-determined overall output or income variable must be consistent with the system's microeconomics.

This, we shall find, is ensured through this overall output or income variable in Model B also taking on the meaning of a budget constraint. This budget constraint, in turn, will provide the basis for the maximizing behavior of the individual and the firm. Hence it is consistent with the system's microeconomic character.

Consequently, our revised classical system, Model B, will have a macroeconomic character in being characterized by a behaviorally-determined overall output or income variable. Yet the system will be a microeconomic system in being based wholly on the behavior of the individual and the firm.

3.9 The Macroeconomic Character Of The New Systems

We have discussed how Model B is characterized by a behaviorally-determined overall output in that it is determined by the operation of the system's market processes. Hence it is determined internally in the system. Next, we have discussed how Model B's budget constraint reflects the system's overall output or income.

Hence Model B's budget constraint is also determined internally in the system by the system's market equilibrating processes. This brings out a basic difference between Model B and orthodox systems such as Model A.

This is because the budget constraints of our new systems, in being determined internally in the systems by the operation of the systems' market equilibrating processes, cannot restrict the systems to any specific states.

Orthodox systems such as Model A, however, are subject to budget constraints that are imposed externally on the systems; and these budget constraints restrict the systems to specific states. These are the states associated with the volume of resources implied by these budget constraints.

This external budget constraint, in the case of Model A, is Say's Law which restricts the system to long-run states. Hence the external budget constraints that are imposed on orthodox systems, in restricting the systems to specific states, suppress the systems' macroeconomic character.

Whereas our new systems are rid of these external budget constraints of orthodox systems in that the new systems are subject to internally-determined budget constraints; and these constraints cannot restrict the systems to any specific states. Hence the systems have a macroeconomic character.

Let us contrast the new and the orthodox systems in the following way. We shall internalize in our new systems, through the systems' internal budget constraints, the external budget constraints that are imposed on orthodox systems but which restrict the latter systems to specific states.

Hence our new systems can move freely among alternative states as behavior changes, unrestricted by externally-imposed budget constraints such as characterize orthodox systems. This reflects how our new systems have a macroeconomic character.

Moreover, these internal budget constraints will be consistent with the systems being wholly microeconomic in character; since these internal budget constraints will provide the basis for the maximizing behavior of the individual and the firm.

As a result, our new systems, while having a macroeconomic character, will be microeconomic systems in being based wholly on the behavior of the individual and the firm.

3.10 Internalizing The External Budget Constraints Of Orthodox Systems

We discussed in the preceding section how we shall internalize in our new systems, the external budget constraints of orthodox systems; and we shall now discuss how this will be accomplished.

Say's Law is imposed externally on Model A to make the system mathematically; and this restricts the system to long-run states. Moreover, the Law is made to act as an externally-imposed budget constraint on the system.

However, as discussed in Section 3.7, we shall collapse the aggregate demand and supply variables in the Say's Law identity into a single variable W. This variable reflects the overall output or income and the budget constraint of both Model A and Model B. However, while W is outside the behavioral content of Model A, we shall find that it enters the behavioral content of Model B.

As a result, Model A's external budget constraint, which is Say's Law, is transformed into a single variable, which is W, that enters the behavioral content of Model B as an internal budget constraint. But exactly why does W take on the meaning of a budget constraint in Model B?

This, we shall find, is because of the new approach to behavior underlying Model B. This behavior, as will be discussed in Chapter 6, is reflected in a new type of demand and supply functions that will characterize Model B; and we shall find that there are internal functions within Model B demand and supply functions.

These internal functions then operate on W to determine the individual quantities of commodities demanded and supplied; and this accounts for W taking on the meaning of a budget constraint in Model B.

Consequently, the external budget constraint of Model A, which is Say's Law, restricts the system to long-run states. However, this external budget constraint is transformed in Model B into a single variable, W, that enters the behavioral content of Model B as an internal budget constraint.

This rids Model B of Model A's external budget constraint that restricts the latter system to long-run states. Hence Model B is not restricted in this way hence the system will move to alternative states as behavior changes.

Moreover, although Model B is rid of Model A's externally-imposed budget constraint, which is Say's Law, we do not lose in Model B the meaning of the Law as a budget constraint. This, to review, is because the variable W into which we transform the Law, enters Model B as an internal budget constraint.

This analysis explains why Model B will have a more general character than the Model A; and this will also have basic implications for the Keynesian system.

To review, we shall bring Model A's external budget constraint, which is Say's Law, into the behavioral content of Model B in the form of the single variable W. This rids Model B of Model A's form of Say's Law that restricts Model A to long-run states. Hence Model B is not restricted in this way.

This gives Model B a macroeconomic character which is reflected in the system being able to move to alternative states as behavior changes.

Moreover, Model B's internal budget constraint that is reflected in the variable W, provides the basis for Model B to have a microeconomic character in every state that the system may describe, states determined by the macroeconomic behavior of the system.

Hence Model B, while having a macroeconomic character, is a microeconomic system in being based wholly on the behavior of the individual and the firm. In contrast, while the Keynesian system also has a macroeconomic character, the microeconomics of the real part of the Keynesian system is suppressed.

3.11 Summary

Model A, the orthodox form of the classical system, was set out in this chapter. The system, as discussed, is initially inconsistent in a mathematical sense. Then it is made mathematically consistent through Say's Law being imposed on the system to eliminate a surplus equation.

However, while generally being taken to be consistent, we found that Model A reflects the economic inconsistency we have uncovered in the system. But through Model B, we shall resolve Model A's economic inconsistency as well as how this inconsistency is reflected in the latter system in mathematical terms.

Finally, in Sections 3.8 to 3.10, we provided some preliminary remarks on the integration of microeconomic and macroeconomic systems in the book as well as preliminary remarks on the macroeconomic character of our new systems. These analyses bring out properties of our price new systems that result from our resolving the inconsistency we have uncovered in the orthodox systems.

Chapter 4

Problems With The Classical And Neoclassical Systems

4.1 Introduction

Keynes has shown that the classical system is restricted to long-run, full-employment states; and he attributed this to Say's Law. While Patinkin held that the neoclassical system is characterized by an invalid dichotomy between its real and monetary sectors that is caused by the "homogeneity postulate."

This, in turn, mars the neoclassical system in other ways, for example, by causing the system's price level to be indeterminate.

These problems do characterize the orthodox forms of the classical and neoclassical systems, systems we both represent by Model A. However, we shall find that they stem from the inconsistency in the systems uncovered in this book, an inconsistency we shall resolve.

Keynes and Patinkin, however, did not uncover and resolve this inconsistency. Instead, their systems are such that they bypass or avoid this inconsistency. Hence they could not resolve these problems in a fully satisfactory manner.

This is reflected in Keynes and Patinkin leaving Model A untouched and hence still characterized by the problems they had uncovered and by incorrect forms of Say's Law and the "homogeneity postulate" that cause these problems.

4.2 Keynes' Criticisms Of The Classical System

Model A, the orthodox form of the classical system, is characterized by Say's Law; and the Law, as Keynes showed, restricts the system to long-run, full-employment states.[13] Say's Law puts the aggregate demand for commodities identical to the aggregate supply; and Keynes took this as reflecting how the classical economists assumed that aggregate demand always

---

[13] J.M.Keynes, *The General Theory Of Employment, Interest And Money* (New York, 1936), esp. Chs. 2 and 3.

automatically adjusts to maintain aggregate supply, or overall real output, at a long-run, full-employment level.

This, in turn, implies that the system possesses a perfectly flexible price mechanism that causes it to always move freely to such a long-run equilibrium. We may also describe the system's market equilibrating processes in the following way.

Say's Law, to review, puts the aggregate demand for commodities identical to the aggregate supply. Hence an excess demand (supply) anywhere in the system will be matched by an equal excess supply (demand) elsewhere in the system.

This, it is then held, causes the relative prices to instantaneously adjust to eliminate this disequilibrium in the various markets of the system without changing overall output. As a result, the system will remain at full-employment although there will, of course, be frictional unemployment, a consequence of job search.

Keynes, however, formed a short-run or macroeconomic system where general unemployment could occur; and to do so, he had to abandon Say's Law and the perfectly flexible classical price mechanism it implies. Keynes then showed that there were various reasons why aggregate demand may be deficient to cause aggregate supply or overall output to fall below a full-employment level.

Hence Keynes regarded his system as being more general than the classical system in that it can describe short-run states that are characterized by general unemployment. Whereas the classical system is restricted to long-run, full-employment states.

4.3 Resolving The Restriction Of The Classical System To Long-Run States

As discussed, Keynes held that the classical system is restricted to long-run states by Say's Law. However, while Model A is restricted in this way, this is due to the hidden economic inconsistency we have uncovered in the system.

This inconsistency arises because Model A's functions do not ensure that the system is consistent with limitation in resources. This is because the aspect to behavior that should ensure that the system is consistent with limitation in resources is missing from the system.

This, in turn, leads to Model A being initially inconsistent in a mathematical sense. Say's Law is then imposed on the system to make it mathematically consistent. Hence the Law is misused in Model A; since it is used in the attempt to make the system, which is inconsistent in an economic sense, consistent by making it mathematically consistent, which is impossible.

Next, this misuse of Say's Law in Model A results in an incorrect or inconsistent form of the Law entering the system; and it is this incorrect Say's Law that restricts Model A to long-run states.

However, in resolving Model A's hidden economic inconsistency through Model B, we shall find that the latter system is automatically consistent in a mathematical sense. Hence we do not need Say's Law to make Model B mathematically consistent.

This, as will be discussed in Chapter 6, results in Model A's incorrect form of Say's Law being replaced in Model B by a correct form of the Law. This, as will be shown in Chapter 9, is a form of the Law that cannot have any influence on Model B in being solely a descriptive device in the system. As a result, it cannot restrict Model B to long-run states.

Consequently, while Model B will describe long-run states, this is because of the long-run behavior we purposefully incorporate into the system through its demand and supply functions. Hence by the same token, we may bring short-run behavior into these functions to cause the system to move into short-run states.

This means that unlike Model A, Model B is not necessarily restricted to long-run states but can move to short-run states were behavior to change. This reflects how Model B has a macroeconomic character even though it is a microeconomic system in being based wholly on the behavior of the individual and the firm.

4.4 Further Remarks On The Restriction Of The Classical System To Long-Run States

Keynes held in his *General Theory* that Say's Law accounts for the existence of the classical system's long-run market processes; and this is also the case with Model A. Moreover, the Law, as we have seen, is required to ensure consistency of Model A.

Hence Model A is consistent only as a long-run system, to explain why the system is necessarily restricted to long-run states. Let us discuss how this will be resolved.

Say's Law, to review, accounts for the existence of Model A's long-run market processes. However, as discussed in the previous section, we shall remove Model A's form of Say's Law from Model B. This results in Model B reflecting a form of the Law that is a true identity.

This is because Model B's Say's Law is simply a descriptive device, as will be confirmed in Chapter 9. Hence it cannot possibly account for the existence of Model B's long-run market processes. Consequently, there is some other means whereby long-run market processes are brought into the latter system; and this indeed is the case.

We shall rid Model B of Model A's form of Say's Law that accounts for the existence of the latter system's long-run market processes. This is by basing Model B on a more general type of demand and supply functions compared to those of Model A.

These new functions, as will be discussed in Chapter 6.5, will account for the existence of long-run market processes in Model B. Hence these processes will be behaviorally-determined in Model B rather than being determined in a non-behavioral manner, as in Model A, by Say's Law.

Moreover, since Model B's long-run market processes are determined by the system's demand and supply functions, these functions may be made to reflect other forms of behavior such as short-run behavior.

As a result, while Model B will reflect long-run behavior, the system will not necessarily be restricted to long-run states. Hence were behavior to change to short-run behavior, Model B will move to a short-run state, a reflection of the system having a macroeconomic character.

4.5 Patinkin's Criticisms Of The Neoclassical System

Keynes emphasized the presence of Say's Law in the classical system and how it restricts the system to long-run, full-employment states. Patinkin, in contrast, focused on the neoclassical system's "homogeneity postulate" which, he showed, mars the system in basic ways.

These are reflected in the neoclassical system which, like the classical system, we represent by Model A, being invalidly dichotomized into real and monetary parts with the system's price level being indeterminate. As well, Walras Law is violated in the system. Patinkin hence concluded that the system is inconsistent.

However, it was later shown by Hickman, Valavanis and a number of other economists that Model A, strictly speaking, is not inconsistent. This is because they showed that Model A may be looked on as being a formally consistent system in that it can be solved for equilibrium; and Patinkin agreed that Model A may be considered in this sense to be consistent an issue.

However, Patinkin held that this issue of the formal mathematical consistency of Model A was not in question and was not relevant to what he held was the main problem with Model A. This is that the system is inconsistent in an economic sense.[14]

This inconsistency, Patinkin held, is reflected in Model A being unable to describe behavior out of equilibrium. Hence the system cannot deal with basic monetary issues such as the stability of monetary equilibrium.

Moreover, Patinkin's criticisms of Model A led him to form his real-balance system where real balances are introduced as a determinant of behavior. Nonetheless, Patinkin's criticism that Model A is inconsistent in an economic sense is of relevance to this book.

This is because we shall see that our solution, through Model B, to the problem of the classical system being restricted to long-run states, implies that Model B is consistent with the existence of market equilibrating processes.

This further implies that Model B resolves the price level indeterminacy and related problems of Model A brought out by Patinkin; and these problems are resolved in the book as will be discussed in Chapter 12.

Hence we shall find that Model A is indeed inconsistent in an economic sense but this is on account of the hidden inconsistency we uncover in the system, an inconsistency that is resolved through Model B. Patinkin, however, did not uncover this inconsistency. As well, the economists who took Model A to be consistent also did not uncover this inconsistency.

4.6 Comments On The Problems With Model A

Keynes showed that the classical system is necessarily restricted to long-run, full-employment states by Say's Law. While Patinkin held that the price level of the neoclassical system is indeterminate, a problem that stems from the system's "homogeneity postulate."

These, however, are problems with the *general logic* of the systems. There are two overall aspects to price systems:

First, the systems each reflect some specific form of behavior say long or short-run behavior. Second, however, the

---

[14] On these issues see Patinkin, *op.cit.,* Ch.VIII and pps. 624-29.

systems should also reflect properties that characterize all price systems or price systems in general.

Clearly, we should include among the latter properties that a system should not necessarily be restricted to any particular state and that a system should possess market equilibrating processes.

Next, since these two properties are taken to be properties that should characterize price systems in general, they stem from the general logic of the systems.

Hence since Keynes found that Model A is necessarily restricted to long-run states, and Patinkin found that the system is also inconsistent with the existence of market processes, Keynes and Patinkin uncovered a fault with the general logic of the system.

However, this fault in the general logic of Model A is a result of the hidden inconsistency we have uncovered in the system. Moreover, since Keynes and Patinkin did not uncover and resolve this inconsistency, their systems are such that they bypass or avoid this inconsistency in their systems.

This allowed them to form their short-run or macroeconomic systems. However, they left the classical and neoclassical systems untouched.

Consequently, they left the latter systems still characterized by the problems they had uncovered and by the incorrect forms of Say's Law and the "homogeneity postulate" that cause these problems. As a result, the Keynesian and Patinkin systems are dichotomized from Model A.

We shall, however, resolve the problems with Model A uncovered by Keynes and Patinkin by resolving their underlying cause, namely, the hidden inconsistency in Model A. This will lead to an approach that correctly captures the general economic logic of price systems; and this will allow us to satisfactorily resolve the problems with Model A that we have described.

4.7 Summary

Keynes held that the classical system is restricted by Say's Law to long-run, full-employment states. While Patinkin held that the "homogeneity postulate" results in the neoclassical system being inconsistent in an economic sense.

However, we shall find that these problems with the classical and neoclassical systems, systems we both represent by Model A, arise because of the hidden inconsistency we have uncovered in the latter system. Keynes and Patinkin, however, did not uncover and resolve this inconsistency hence their systems bypass Model A's inconsistency.

Consequently, they left Model A untouched and hence characterized by the problems they had uncovered and by incorrect forms of Say's Law and the "homogeneity postulate" that cause these problems.

We shall, however, resolve Model A's hidden inconsistency that is the underlying cause of these problems; and this will allow us to satisfactorily resolve the problems with Model A that we have described.

Chapter 5

The Rationale Of The New Approach To Price Systems

5.1 Introduction

Overall, we may look on the book as generalizing the orthodox classical system, Model A, through Model B, our revised classical system; and in the process, we shall also generalize the Keynesian system by giving the latter system a satisfactory microeconomic character.

We shall generalize Model A through Model B by bringing a more general approach to microeconomics into the latter system. Moreover, we shall find that unlike Model A, Model B is not restricted to long-run states. Hence Model B can move into short-run states were behavior to change.

This means that short-run or macroeconomic systems emerge from Model B; and these short-run systems, like Model B, will also have a satisfactory microeconomic character. Whereas the Keynesian macroeconomic system is an alternative to the classical microeconomic system with the microeconomics of the Keynesian system being largely suppressed.

5.2 Removing A Barrier To Integrating Microeconomic And Macroeconomic Systems

We shall, as will be discussed in Section 5.4 below, elicit from the microeconomic Model A a macroeconomic variable, W, that reflects the long-run overall output or income of the system; and we shall find that this variable is determined in a non-behavioral manner. This confirms Keynes' view that the classical system is restricted to long-run states.

However, if we leave Model A at this stage, we would have to proceed like Keynes to form a macroeconomic system that is an alternative to Model A. But this is an approach that creates a barrier between Model A and the Keynesian system, to dichotomize the systems.

This barrier, however, will be removed by Model B on account of a more general approach to microeconomics underlying the latter system. This will allow us to go beyond forming a macroeconomic system that is an alternative to Model A.

Instead, we shall be able to form a system, Model B, that has a simultaneous microeconomic-macroeconomic character, a system that will hence form the basis to integrate microeconomic and macroeconomic systems. Let us sketch how this will be accomplished.

There is a behaviorally-determined overall output or income in the Keynesian system; and we shall find that this is also the case with Model B. This reflects how both systems have a macroeconomic character.

Next, we shall denote the behaviorally-determined overall output or income of both systems by W. This variable is a summation, in a common unit, of the individual quantities of commodities determined in the systems. We shall find, however, that the overall output or income variable W differs significantly between the Keynesian system and Model B.

Clearly, the Keynesian W abstracts from or suppresses the microeconomic market processes of the real part of the Keynesian system. This is because the Keynesian W directly enters the market processes of the Keynesian system where it is determined by aggregate demand and supply functions.

Hence individual quantities of commodities, and the commodity relative prices, are not determined. This reflects how the Keynesian system abstracts from or suppresses the microeconomics of the real part of the system.

Model B, however, is quite different since the variable W in the system is consistent with the existence of microeconomic market processes. To show this, we must provide a sketch of the rational behavior underlying Model B although this rational behavior will be covered in detail in Chapter 6.9.

We shall find that the rational behavior of Model B is reflected in individuals and firms determining their commodity demands and supplies in the knowledge or awareness that their resources are limited. Hence there is utility to individuals and firms of a variable that reflects their overall resources.

This gives rise to an aggregative variable that reflects their limited resources or budget constraint; and we shall take this variable in Model B as reflecting a summation in a common unit of the current flow of the individual quantities of commodities that are determined in the system.

This means that this aggregative variable that we take as reflecting the limited resources or budget constraint of individuals and firms in Model B is the same variable W of Model B, that was introduced earlier, that reflects the overall output or income of the system; since the latter W is also a summation of the current flow of the individual quantities of commodities that are determined in the system.

Hence the overall output or income of Model B reflects the system's limited resources or budget constraint. We may now see why the microeconomic character of the real part of the Keynesian system is suppressed whereas Model B is a wholly microeconomic system.

We have discussed how the overall output or income variable W of the Keynesian system directly enters the market processes of the system where it is determined by aggregate demand and supply functions. However, these functions suppress the individual quantities of commodities and the commodity relative prices.

This reflects how the Keynesian W abstracts from the microeconomics of the real part of the Keynesian system. On the other hand, the W of Model B does not directly enter the market processes of the system. Hence the system's microeconomic market processes are not suppressed.

Instead, we shall find that the overall output or income variable W of Model B enters the system *as a budget constraint,* causing it to enter the system's demand and supply functions.

Next, we shall find in Chapter 6 that functions that are interior to Model B's demand and supply functions operate on W to determine individual quantities of commodities demanded and supplied. These individual quantities then enter the markets of the system reflecting how the system has a microeconomic character.

Consequently, the overall output or income variable W of Model B has a meaning of relevance to both macroeconomic and microeconomic systems. To review, the variable W of Model B, in reflecting the system's overall output or income, is relevant to macroeconomic systems.

However, as we have discussed, the variable W of Model B also simultaneously reflects the system's limited resources or budget constraint. Hence it is also relevant to microeconomic systems since it will provide the basis for the maximizing behavior of the individual and the firm.

As a result, the variable W of Model B is relevant to both macroeconomic and microeconomic systems. This will account for Model B having a dual microeconomic-macroeconomic character; and this will result in the system providing the basis to integrate microeconomic and macroeconomic systems.

On the other hand, the overall output or income variable W of the Keynesian system has a meaning of relevance only to macroeconomic systems. This suppresses the microeconomics of the real part of the Keynesian system, with the individual quantities of commodities and the commodity relative prices hence being suppressed. Let us go further into these issues.

5.3 Model B's Internal Logic Transforms Overall Output Or Income Into A Budget Constraint

Clearly, a key aspect to Model B lies in the system's overall output or income W also becoming an internally-determined budget constraint in the system. Let us go further into this which requires discussing in an overall way, how macroeconomic systems are formed.

We earlier set out a condition for internal consistency of a macroeconomic system; and we shall now discuss this condition in more detail.

To form a macroeconomic system, the system must first be able, in principle, to move among alternative states as behavior changes. This requires that the system be rid of Model A's form of Say's Law that restricts the latter system to long-run states.

Moreover, there must be a market process or mechanism that ensures that the system actually moves to alternative states as behavior changes. This is ensured by the system being characterized by a behaviorally-determined overall output or income variable.

Let us now set out, first in general terms, our condition for internal consistency of a macroeconomic system.

This is that the way in which the system is rid of Model A's Say's Law must be consistent with the nature of the system's overall output or income variable. This is our condition for internal consistency of a macroeconomic system. Let us, however, now put this condition into a form that makes it relevant to specific systems.

This is that if we rid a system of Model A's Say's Law through macroeconomic analysis, the system's overall output must be consistent with macroeconomic analysis. By the same token, if we rid a system of Model A's Say's Law through microeconomic analysis, the system's overall output variable must be consistent with microeconomic analysis.

This is our condition for internal consistency of a macroeconomic system when this condition is put in a way that makes it relevant to specific systems. Let us now consider Keynes' approach to forming his macroeconomic system in the context of this condition for internal consistency of a macroeconomic system.

Say's Law restricts the classical system, Model A, to long-run states. Next, Keynes removed Model A's form of the Law from his system; but this was through macroeconomic analysis. This is reflected in Keynes allowing aggregate demand and supply to diverge. Hence Keynes' system, in principle, can move to alternative states.

This, in turn, gives a macroeconomic character to the actual means whereby the system is made to move to alternative states; and this is reflected in Keynes' overall output variable W being macroeconomic in character.

This is in the sense that it only carries the meaning of the Keynesian system's overall output. Hence the Keynesian system meets our condition for internal consistency of macroeconomic systems but though macroeconomic analysis.

Let us now consider Model B; and we shall find that this system also meets this condition. Yet Model B is more general than the Keynesian system. This is because Model B meets our condition for internal consistency of a macroeconomic system through microeconomic analysis. This is through our resolving the inconsistency we have uncovered within Model A through Model B.

We shall thereby base the latter system on a more general approach to microeconomics; and this results in Model B being rid of Model A's incorrect form of Say's Law that restricts the latter system to long-run states. Hence it is through microeconomic analysis that Model B, in principle, is made able to move among alternative states.

Next, Model B, like the Keynesian system, must also be characterized by a behaviorally-determined overall output or income variable W. However, the W in Model B must now be consistent with the microeconomic approach whereby we rid Model B of Model A's Say's Law; and we shall find that this is indeed the case.

This is through W entering the behavioral content of Model B as a budget constraint. Then the functions of Model B that rid the system of Say's Law operate on the W in Model B to determine individual quantities of commodities demanded and supplied.

This reflects how the overall output or income variable W of Model B's is consistent with the system's microeconomic character. Hence it is consistent with how the system, in the first place, was made consistent, in principle, with having a macroeconomic character through microeconomic analysis.

5.4 Eliciting An Overall Output Variable In Model A

Model A, the orthodox classical system, is shown again below:

Model A

1. $D_j \equiv F_j [z]$

2. $S_j \equiv G_j [z]$

3. $E_j [z] = 0$

Say's Law is also shown below:

4. $ad \equiv as$

Say's Law, to review, puts the aggregate demand for commodities identical to the aggregate supply. This means that, taking the Law as indeed a true identity, we may collapse the aggregate demand and supply variables in (4) into a single variable; and we denote this latter variable by W.

This variable is derived by measuring the individual quantities of commodities determined in the system in a common unit then summing them.

Clearly, the variable W represents the current flow of overall output or income of Model A in terms of commodities. This is because the individual quantities of commodities that are determined in the system must necessarily sum to W.

Hence we are also using W to represent the overall output or income of Model A as we did in the case of Model B and the Keynesian system; and like Model B, the overall output variable W of Model A, as we shall now discuss, also reflects the latter system's limited resources or budget constraint.

Say's Law is imposed on Model A to make the system mathematically consistent; and the Law imposes W on the system, this variable reflecting the overall output or income of the system.

Next, we discussed earlier how in making Model A mathematically consistent, we may solve for the system's equilibrium quantities and prices; and the equilibrium quantities must sum to a limited volume of resources underlying the system.

Moreover, these quantities also sum to the variable W which is why we could, in the first place, look on W as reflecting the overall output of the system. Hence since the quantities we solve for must sum to a limited volume of resources, this limited volume of resources is W.

Consequently, Model A's overall output or income also reflects the system's limited resources or budget constraint. Hence Model A and Model B are similar in that the overall output or income variable W in both systems also reflects the systems' limited resources or budget constraints.

Nonetheless, there is a key difference between the systems which will explain why Model B is more general than Model A. This is reflected in their being a different explanation in the two systems for why overall output or income of the systems also reflects the systems' limited resources or budget constraint.

We have discussed in Section 5.2 how the identification of Model B's overall output or income with the system's limited resources or budget constraint is due to the rational behavior underlying the system.

On the other hand, Model A lacks the rational behavior of Model B. Hence while the overall output or income of Model A also reflects the system's limited resources or budget constraint, this is not ensured, as in Model B, by the rational behavior of individuals and firms.

Instead, this relationship is ensured in Model A in a non-behavioral manner as a result of the system being made mathematically consistent by Say's Law. Whereas it is ensured in Model B by the rational behavior that characterizes the system.

We shall now discuss how Model A is made consistent with limitation in resources in a manner that will provide a clue as to the nature of the new type of demand and supply functions that will characterize Model B.

5.5 How Model A Is Made Consistent With Limitation in Resources

Model A, the orthodox classical system, appears again below:

Model A

1. $\quad D_j \equiv F_j\left[z\right]$

2. $\quad S_j \equiv G_j\left[z\right]$

3. $\quad E_j\left[z\right] \equiv 0$

Next, we also show below the Say's Law identity which is imposed on Model A to make the system mathematically consistent. This identity, to review, puts the aggregate demand for commodities identical to the aggregate supply:

4. $\qquad ad \equiv as$

We shall be using the variable W in the following analyses, this variable, to review, reflecting both the overall output or income of Model A as well as the system's limited resources or budget constraint.

As well, we bear in mind that W was formed by our collapsing the aggregate demand and supply variables in (4) into this single variable. Hence both aggregate demand and supply are identical to W.

There are n demand functions in expression (1) of Model A that determine n quantities demanded. However, for these n quantities to sum to W or to aggregate demand in the Say's Law identity, expression (4), we must proceed in the following way.

We first take $(n{-}1)$ quantities demanded from $(n{-}1)$ demand functions and substitute them into W. Then we take the difference between W and the sum of the $(n{-}1)$ quantities to determine the nth quantity. Hence this n^{th} quantity is determined as a residual which means that the nth demand function becomes redundant.

Next, we may take every quantity demanded successively as the nth quantity. This means that we may look on every quantity as being successively determined as a residual.

As a result, any one demand function can be looked on as being redundant, the demand functions hence being reduced to being $(n-1)$ in number. Let us now look at this analysis from a somewhat different perspective.

We may, as was discussed, look on the nth quantity demanded as being determined as a residual.

This means that this n^{th} quantity is adjusted *relatively* to the other $(n-1)$ quantities so that all n quantities may sum to W or to ad in (4).

Next, since we may take every quantity successively as the nth quantity, this means that we may look on every quantity as being successively adjusted relatively to the remaining $(n-1)$ quantities so that all n quantities may always sum to W or to ad in expression (4).

Hence the quantities demanded in Model A are *relative* quantities; and this explains why they are always consistent with the system's budget constraint. This, of course, is because they can adjust in a relative manner so as to always sum to W or to ad in expression (4).

Clearly, also, redundancy of any one demand function in Model A is a consequence of the quantities demanded being transformed into relative quantities.

We may also apply this analysis in a generally similar manner to the supply side of Model A. This is to show that the quantities supplied are also *relative* quantities and that this explains why they are always consistent with the system's budget constraint.

This is because the quantities supplied, in being relative quantities, will also adjust in a relative manner so as to always sum to W or to as in (4).

Moreover, continuing to follow the analysis on the demand side, any one supply function in Model A also becomes redundant, a result of quantities supplied being transformed into relative quantities.

Hence Model A is made consistent with limitation in resources by the quantities demanded being transformed into relative quantities demanded and by the quantities supplied being transformed into relative quantities supplied; and this is a result of the system being made mathematically consistent by Say's Law. Let us go further into this analysis.

5.6 Model A Is Made Consistent With Limited Resources By Being Made Mathematically Consistent

We discussed in Chapter 2.2 how Model A is made consistent with limitation in resources as a consequence of the system being made mathematically consistent. However, this will now be established in a manner that provides a clue, to be discussed in the following section, as to the form of our new type of demand and supply functions.

As discussed, the quantities demanded (supplied) must be transformed into relative quantities demanded (supplied) in price systems in order to ensure that these quantities always sum to the limited volume of resources of the systems.

This is because these quantities, in being relative quantities, will adjust in a relative manner so as to always add up to the total of the systems' limited resources. Model A's orthodox-type functions, however, initially determine absolute quantities.

Hence these quantities will not initially sum to the system's limited volume of resources. This means that these quantities must be transformed into relative quantities to make them always sum to the limited volume of resources of the system. This is accomplished in Model A by the system being made mathematically consistent.

To review, economists impose Say's Law, the identity $ad \equiv as$ on Model A, to make the system mathematically consistent through eliminating a surplus equation. We also saw that we may replace the Say's Law identity with the single variable, W.

This variable, to review, represents the overall long-run output or income of the system; and as well, it represents the limited resources or budget constraint of the system.

Clearly, the quantities demanded (supplied) will always automatically sum to W only if they are transformed into relative quantities demanded (supplied). This is because they can then adjust in a relative manner to always sum to W.

However, the simple imposing of W on the system cannot transform quantities into relative quantities. Let us review how quantities are, in fact, transformed into relative quantities in Model A.

Since Model A initially determines absolute rather than relative quantities, the system is initially inconsistent with limited resources. This is because these quantities will not necessarily sum to W. This, in turn, causes the system to be inconsistent in a mathematical sense which is reflected in there being a surplus equation over the number of unknowns.

Economists then make the system mathematically consistent by eliminating this surplus equation; and this, as we shall now discuss, transforms quantities into relative quantities.

Model A's surplus equation is eliminated by economists imposing Say's Law on the system which also imposes W on the system. Hence through imposing W on Model A, we eliminate a surplus equation; and this, of course, eliminates one quantity demanded and one quantity supplied.

Next, in eliminating one quantity demanded and one quantity supplied, we transform the quantities demanded (supplied) into relative quantities demanded (supplied) along the lines discussed in the previous section.

That is, we may look on the elimination of the nth quantity demanded (supplied) as reflecting how this quantity demanded (supplied) is made to adjust relatively to the remaining $(n-1)$ quantities demanded (supplied) to allow all n quantities demanded (supplied) to sum to W.

We may then, as was also discussed in the previous section, take each quantity demanded (supplied) successively as the nth quantity demanded (supplied) to illustrate how every quantity, in being successively eliminated, is made to adjust relatively to the remaining $(n-1)$ quantities. This allows all n quantities demanded (supplied) to sum to W.

As a result, the quantities demanded (supplied) are transformed into relative quantities demanded (supplied) in Model A.

Hence it is through our making Model A mathematically consistent by imposing Say's Law on the system to eliminate a surplus equation, that we make the system consistent with limitation in resources. However, this is through mathematical consistency transforming quantities into relative quantities.

That is, the process whereby we eliminate a surplus equation to make Model A mathematically consistent transforms quantities into relative quantities. Then it is this transformation of quantities into relative quantities that ensures that these quantities always sum to W to make the system consistent with limitation in resources.

This analysis provides a clue as to the form of a new type of demand and supply functions that will resolve the hidden inconsistency of Model A.

5.7 The New Type Of Demand And Supply Functions

An economic inconsistency enters Model A because consistency with limited resources is not ensured by the system's behavior or economic rationale.

This is because Model A's functions, and hence the behavior in the system, does not ensure that the system is consistent with limitation in resources. Instead, consistency with limited resources is ensured as a consequence of the system being made mathematically consistent.

Next, we found that this is through the quantities being transformed into relative quantities due to the system being made mathematically consistent. This provides us with a clue as to how Model A's hidden inconsistency may be resolved.

Since mathematical consistency ensures consistency of Model A with limited resources by transforming quantities into relative quantities, this raises the possibility that there may be a way to avoid having to use mathematical consistency to ensure that Model A is consistent with limited resources.

That is, some way other than through making the system mathematically consistent to transform quantities into relative quantities. This new way is through making the system's demand and supply functions themselves determine relative quantities of commodities demanded and relative quantities supplied.

This leads to the new type of demand and supply functions to be set out in this book, functions to be called *relative demand and supply functions*.

This is because these functions, to be set out formally in the next chapter, will determine *relative* quantities of commodities demanded and *relative* quantities of commodities supplied. Moreover, these relative quantities demanded and relative quantities supplied will be made to depend only on the relative prices.

These new demand and supply functions will become the basis for Model B, our revised form of Model A. Hence through Model B, we shall resolve the economic inconsistency of Model A; since Model B's functions will ensure that the system is consistent with limitation in resources.

This is because the system's functions will determine relative quantities of commodities demanded and relative quantities supplied. Hence the quantities determined by the functions, in being relative quantities, will adjust in a relative manner to always sum to the limited volume of resources in the system.

As a result, consistency with limitation in resources will be ensured in Model B by the behavior or economic rationale of the system, in being ensured by the system's demand and supply functions. This reflects how through Model B, we shall resolve the hidden economic inconsistency of Model A.

Moreover, we shall thereby also resolve how this inconsistency is reflected in Model A in mathematical terms.

5.8 An Alternative Way Of Deriving The New Type Of Demand And Supply Functions

We have discussed one means through which we came upon our new type of demand and supply functions. Let us now, however, discuss another way in which we may arrive at these new functions. This is an approach that traces explicitly, through Say's Law, directly to the classical system.

Say's Law in Model A puts the aggregate demand for commodities identical to the aggregate supply. This means that any excess demand (supply) anywhere in the system will be matched by an equal excess supply (demand) elsewhere in the system.

Hence it is also usually concluded that the relative prices will instantaneously adjust to eliminate this disequilibrium in the various markets of the system without changing overall output. This means that the system remains at full-employment although there will be frictional unemployment, a consequence of job search.

This is a description of a long-run market equilibrating process that ensures general equilibrium of Model A. That is, a process that ensures that every individual market is cleared in the long-run.

Let us now, as we did in Section 5.4, again collapse the aggregate demand and supply variables in the Say's Law identity into the single variable W. This implies that we are taking the Law as a true identity hence it can have no substantive influence in the system.

Next, the variable W, to review, reflects the long-run overall output or income of Model A; and it also represents the budget constraint or limited resources of the system.

Clearly, when taking W to reflect the limited resources of the system, as we shall now do, we must necessarily take it to be fixed. This means that we must also take the aggregate demand and supply of commodities to be fixed since both are identical to the fixed W.

Hence since the aggregate demand and supply of commodities are both fixed, what adjusts in response to the relative prices in the market processes described, are the *relative* quantities of commodities demanded and the *relative* quantities of commodities supplied.

This provides another way of arriving at our long-run relative demand and supply functions; since it implies that we must write functions that make the relative quantities of commodities demanded (supplied) depend only on the relative prices.

Moreover, this approach to forming our relative demand and supply functions traces explicitly, through Say's Law, directly to the classical system. This will be a key factor in explaining later in the book, in Chapter 13, why we shall take Model B as a classical system.

5.9 An Outline Of The New Approach To Price Systems

Basic to our new approach to price systems is the rational behavior that underlies Model B, the system we use to represent our new systems.

Through this approach to rational behavior, we shall first rid Model B of an incorrect form of Say's Law that restricts Model A to long-run states. This is because, as will be discussed in Chapter 6.7, the behavioral character of Model B rids the latter system's Say's Law of invalid elements and an invalid role that characterize the Law in Model A.

This will account for Model B reflecting a correct form of the Law. This is a form of the Law which, as will be confirmed in Chapter 9, cannot possibly restrict Model B to long-run states. Hence Model B will move to short-run states were behavior to change to short-run behavior.

This will give Model B a macroeconomic character yet the system will be based wholly on microeconomic behavior. This is because the system's macroeconomic character is consistent with the system being a microeconomic system.

Thus since Model B can move to alterative states, the system, like the Keynesian system, has a behaviorally determined overall output or income; and we denoted the overall output or income of both systems by W.

However, the W of the Keynesian system directly enters the market processes of the system; and this abstracts from or suppresses the microeconomic market processes in the real part of the system. Whereas the W of Model B is consistent with the existence of microeconomic market processes in the system.

To review, the rational behavior of individuals and firms in Model B is reflected in them determining their commodity demands and supply in the knowledge or awareness that their resources are limited. As a result, there is utility to individuals and firms of a variable that reflects their overall resources.

This leads to the existence of a variable W that reflects the system's overall output or income as well as the limited resources or budget constraint of individuals and firms. This brings out a basic difference between Model B and the Keynesian system.

While the variable W of Model B reflects the overall output or income of the system, it does not directly enter the markets of the system as in the Keynesian system. Were this the case, the W of Model B would suppress the microeconomic market processes of the system just as the W of the Keynesian system suppresses the microeconomic market processes of the real part of the Keynesian system.

Instead, the overall output or income variable W of Model B, on account of the rational behavior of individuals and firms, also reflects the limited resources or budget constraint of the system; and it enters Model B as a budget constraint, resulting in it entering the system's demand and supply functions.

Next, within Model B's demand and supply functions we shall find the interior functions that we referred to earlier. These operate on the budget constraint W that is also within Model B's functions, to determine individual quantities of commodities demanded and supplied.

These then enter the markets of the system, reflecting how the system has a microeconomic character. Yet the system, as we have discussed earlier, also has a macroeconomic character.

Consequently, while Model B has a macroeconomic character, its macroeconomic character is consistent with the system being a microeconomic system in that Model B is based wholly on the behavior of the individual and the firm.

This explains why Model B provides the basis to integrate microeconomic and macroeconomic systems.

5.10 The Limited Resources Or Budget Constraints Of The New Systems

Underlying our revised classical system, Model B, is an approach to behavior reflected in individuals and firms being taken to be aware that their resources are limited and hence they act in light of this awareness.

Clearly, this approach to behavior is relevant not only to our new systems but to price systems in general. Moreover, we shall find in Chapter 6.9 that this behavior translates into an approach to rational behavior that hence also applies to price systems in general.

However, we have restricted the limited resources or budget constraint of individuals and firms in Model B to reflect the system's overall output or income as reflected in the current flow of commodities in the system.

This has been done to assist us in showing how, through our new approach to price systems, as reflected in Model B, we integrate microeconomic and macroeconomic systems. However, we may form more detailed and complex forms of Model B, that include short-run systems, where the resources of individuals and firms are more broadly defined.

This is to include, for example, stocks of goods and other assets. Nonetheless, our new approach to behavior, and the rational behavior into which this behavior translates, would also apply to these more detailed and complex systems.

5.11 Summary

This chapter discussed how we shall generalize the orthodox classical system, Model A, through Model B, our revised classical system. This is through our bringing into Model B, a more general approach to microeconomics compared to Model A.

Moreover, we shall find that unlike Model A, Model B is not restricted to long-run states but can move into short-run states were behavior to change. As a result, short-run or macroeconomic systems emerge from Model B. Hence like the latter system, these short-run systems will also have a satisfactory microeconomic character.

We shall be able to generalize the classical system in the manner described, through Model B, because we shall introduce into the microeconomic Model B, a macroeconomic variable, W, that reflects the overall output or income of the system. This gives the system a macroeconomic character.

As well, on account of the rational behavior of Model B, the variable W also reflects the system's limited resources or budget constraint; and this budget constraint is consistent with the microeconomic character of the system in providing the basis for the maximizing behavior of the individual and the firm.

This results in Model B, while having a macroeconomic character, yet being a microeconomic system in being based wholly on the behavior of the individual and the firm. Hence Model B provides the basis to integrate microeconomic and macroeconomic systems.

Clearly, a key part of the chapter is reflected in our showing in Section 5.3, that the overall output or income of Model B, on account of the internal logic of the system, also reflects the system's limited resources or budget constraint. There was a key consequence of this for the macroeconomic character and budget constraints of our new systems.

Since the overall output of Model B is determined by the system's market processes, the system's budget constraint, in being reflected in this overall output, is also determined by the system's market processes. Hence Model B is characterized by an internally-determined budget constraint that cannot restrict the system to any particular state.

On the other hand, Model A is subject to an externally-imposed budget constraint, which is Say's Law, that restricts the system to a long-run state. This suppresses the system's macroeconomic character.

However, Model B, in being subject to an internally-determined budget constraint, is not restricted in this way. Hence Model B can move to alternative states as behavior changes, reflecting how the system has a macroeconomic character. These issues are covered in fuller detail in Chapter 10.

Chapter 6

Revision Of The Orthodox Classical System

6.1 Introduction

We described earlier the hidden inconsistency in Model A, the orthodox form of the classical price system, and the problems caused by this inconsistency. As well, we discussed in the preceding chapter how this inconsistency will be resolved. This is through a revision of the orthodox or neoclassical-type demand and supply functions such as characterize Model A.

Revision of the functions will be formally carried out in this chapter. This leads to our new type of demand and supply functions that form the basis for Model B, our revised version of the classical system.

Next, through Model B, we shall resolve the hidden inconsistency of Model A. Moreover, we shall find that Model B is rid of an incorrect form of Say's Law that characterizes Model A and which restricts the latter system to long-run states.

Consequently, Model B is not necessarily restricted to long-run states hence the system will move to short-run states were behavior to change. As a result, Model B has a macroeconomic character. Yet the system is a microeconomic system in being based wholly on the behavior of the individual and the firm.

Finally, the chapter covers in detail the new aspect to rational behavior underlying our new systems and how this accounts for us resolving the issue of Say's Law.

6.2 Comments On The Revised Classical System

Model B, our revised classical system, like Model A, is also a long-run, stationary system with change being ruled out leading to "static expectations." Hence like Model A, it is also assumed in Model B that because of the assumption of the absence of change, individuals and firms will expect that current prices will continue to rule in the future.[15]

Nonetheless, while Model A and B are similar in that both are long-run systems, they differ significantly in terms of their general logic.

Model B's general logic arises from our new conceptual approach to price systems. This approach reflects how we bring into our new systems, the aspect to the behavior of individuals and firms we described in Chapter 2.3 that is missing from the orthodox systems.

This, in turn, leads to a new way of looking at the quantities of goods in price systems, namely, that these quantities must be taken to be relative quantities.

Next, we capture this through our new type of demand and supply functions of Model B that determine relative quantities of commodities demanded and relative quantities supplied. Hence these quantities, in being relative quantities, will adjust in a relative manner to always sum to the total of Model B's limited resources.

Consequently, our relative demand and supply functions of Model B will ensure that the system, which is our revised classical system, is consistent with limitation in resources or a budget constraint.

As a result, these new functions will correctly reflect economic behavior in reflecting behavior that is consistent with limitation in resources; and this will resolve the hidden economic inconsistency of Model A, the orthodox classical system.

6.3 Relative Demand And Supply Functions

Model B's demand and supply functions will make *relative* quantities of commodities demanded and *relative* quantities of commodities supplied, depend on the relative prices. These functions also depend on other variables which are held fixed and hence will not be shown explicitly. These are the same variables as those of Model A.

Among them are the tastes and preferences of individuals and firms as well as their resources. Moreover, population and the state of technology are also held fixed. Let us proceed to form our relative demand and supply functions.

---

[15] On "static expectations" see, for example, O. Lange, *Price Flexibility And Employment* (Bloomington, 1945), pps. 1 and 22.

As in Model A, there are n quantities of commodities in our revised classical system, Model B. As well, we shall continue to denote the quantities of commodities demanded by D_j and the quantities supplied by S_j, where $j=1,2,3,...,n$.

We now take the ratios of the quantities of commodities demanded and the ratios of the quantities of commodities supplied. Next, we denote these ratios, which are each $(n-1)$ in number, by r and s, respectively.

The quantities of commodities must, of course, be measured in a common unit in order to determine the ratios of these quantities.

Next, shown below are what we shall refer to as interior functions, functions we mentioned in Chapter 5. These make the ratios of the quantities of commodities demanded, the r, and the ratios of the quantities of commodities supplied, the s, depend on the relative prices that are represented by the z:

5. $r \equiv f(z)$

6. $s \equiv g(z)$

We then use these interior functions to form Model B's demand and supply functions which are shown below:

7. $D_j \equiv F_j'[f(z)]$

8. $S_j \equiv G_j'[g(z)]$

Underlying these functions is a budget constraint which we represent by Say's Law. This constraint sets the overall or aggregate demand for commodities that individuals and firms can demand, as well as the overall or aggregate supply of commodities that individuals and firms can supply.

Moreover, we have discussed how functions $f(z)$ and $g(z)$ determine the ratios of the quantities of commodities demanded and the ratios of the quantities of commodities supplied, respectively.

Hence functions $f(z)$, together with the overall volume of commodities that individuals and firms can demand that is set by the budget constraint, determine the D_j in (7).

Also, functions $g(z)$, together with the overall volume of commodities that individuals and firms can supply that is also set by the budget constraint, determine the S_j in (8). This analysis illustrates a key property of Model B.

This is that the behavior in the system leads to quantities of commodities demanded and supplied that always necessarily sum to the limited resources or budget constraint of the system. This is a reflection of our bringing the aspect to behavior we described earlier into the system.

This, to review, is the aspect to behavior that ensures that a price system is consistent with limitation in resources.

6.4 Consistency Of The Revised Classical System

We introduced Model B's demand and supply functions, functions (7) and (8), in the preceding section. Let us now use these functions to form Model B's excess-demand equations, which are equations (9).

These latter equations, together with functions (7) and (8), form the overall Model B which is shown below, this being our revised form of the classical system:

Model B

7. $\quad D_j \equiv F_j'[f(z)]$

8. $\quad S_j \equiv G_j'[g(z)]$

9. $\quad E_j'[f(z)-g(z)=0]=0$

Let us assume that Model B is in general equilibrium which is reflected in the overall or external conditions $E_j'[\ ] = 0$ in (9) vanishing. This is only possible if the internal conditions $f(z)-g(z)=0$ simultaneously vanish.

Next, the latter conditions are $(n-1)$ in number hence they are just equal to the number of variables to be determined which are the $(n-1)$ relative prices, the z. This means that Model B is automatically consistent in a mathematical sense.

We shall now discuss why conditions $f(z)-g(z)=0$ vanish in general equilibrium which will allow us to bring out more fully the nature of the equilibrium conditions of the system.

In general equilibrium, the quantity demanded in each market across the system equals the quantity supplied in that market. This necessarily means that in general equilibrium, the ratios of the quantities demanded across the system equal the corresponding ratios of the quantities supplied across the system.

As a result, the system is characterized by $(n-1)$ equilibrium conditions reflecting equality between the ratios of the quantities of commodities demanded across the system with the ratios of the quantities supplied.

Next, functions $f(z)$ determine the ratios of the quantities of commodities demanded across the system. While functions $g(z)$ determine the ratios of the quantities supplied across the system. Hence we may substitute functions $f(z)$ and $g(z)$ into the equilibrium conditions described to form conditions $f(z)-g(z)=0$.

Consequently, when general equilibrium prevails, that is, when the overall conditions $E'_j [\ ] = 0$ in (9) vanish, the conditions $f(z)-g(z)=0$ that are within (9) simultaneously vanish. Moreover, conditions $f(z)-g(z)=0$, to review, are $(n-1)$ in number.

Hence they are just equal to the number of variables to be determined which are the $(n-1)$ relative prices, the z. As a result, unlike Model A, Model B is automatically consistent in a mathematical sense. There is a key implication of this for Say's Law.

Since Model B is automatically consistent in a mathematical sense, we do not need Say's Law to make the system consistent. Hence Model B is rid of what is an incorrect form of the Law that characterizes Model A

Say's Law is an identity hence no substantive role should be attributed to it. Yet the Law is used in Model A to make the system consistent by making it mathematically consistent. This gives the Law a substantive role in Model A to explain why there is an incorrect form of the Law in the system.

However, no such role is given to the Law in Model B since it is not required to make the latter system consistent; since we saw that Model B is automatically consistent in a mathematical sense. Hence Model B is rid of Model A's incorrect form of Say's Law.

We shall now set out a more detailed form of Model B, to be called Model B", that will assist us in bringing out the behavioral character of the system. Moreover, Model B" will allow us to show that Model B is characterized by long-run market processes that stem from the behavior in the system as reflected in the system's demand and supply functions.

Whereas. as was discussed in Chapter 4.4, Model A's long-run market processes owe their existence to a non-behavioral element, Say's Law.

6.5 A More Detailed Form Of The Revised Classical System

We show Model B, our revised classical system, again below:

Model B

7. $D_j \equiv F_j'[f(z)]$

8. $S_j \equiv G_j'[g(z)]$

9. $E_j'[f(z)-g(z)=0]=0$

Say's Law is also shown below:

4. $ad \equiv as$

We next enter the aggregate demand (ad) and aggregate supply (as) variables from the Say's Law identity into Model B to transform the system into Model B' below:

Model B'

7'. $D_j = F_j'[ad, f(z)]$

8'. $S_j \equiv G_j'[as, g(z)]$

9'. $E_j'[(ad \equiv as), f(z) - g(z) = 0] = 0$

Let us now, as we did in Chapter 5.4, collapse the aggregate demand (ad) and aggregate supply (as) variables in the Say's Law identity into the single variable W .

This variable reflects the overall long-run output or income of the system; and W, as well, also reflects the limited resources or budget constraint of the system. We next transform the aggregate demand (ad) and aggregate supply (as) variables in Model B' into the single variable W . Hence we put the system in the form of Model B" below:

Model B"

7". $D_j \equiv F_j'[W, f(z)]$

8". $S_j \equiv G_j'[W, g(z)]$

9". $E_j'[W, f(z) - g(z) = 0] = 0$

Model B" is simply a more detailed form of Model B since through Model B", we have only made the budget constraint of Model B explicit. Hence the systems are interchangeable and we shall use either one depending on which is most useful for the purpose at hand. Moreover, when it assists our discussion, we shall drop the superscript from Model B". Let us now review the latter system.

Functions $f(z)$ and $g(z)$ determine the ratios of the quantities of commodities demanded and the ratios of the quantities supplied, respectively. We also bear in mind, in light of how W was formed, that we may refer to W as either aggregate demand or aggregate supply of commodities.

Let us now take W to reflect aggregate demand as set by the system's budget constraint, W hence being the total volume of commodities that individuals and firms can demand. This means that functions $f(z)$ with W determine the quantities demanded, the D_j, in (7"). There is a generally similar analysis on the supply side.

We now take W to reflect aggregate supply as set by the system's budget constraint, W hence also now being the total volume of commodities that individuals and firms can supply. This means that functions $g(z)$ with W determine the quantities supplied, the S_j, in (8").

As a result, the quantities demanded and the quantities supplied are both necessarily consistent with limitation in resources. This is because they each always sum to W which, as was discussed in Chapter 5, also reflects the system's limited resources or budget constraint.

Hence our new approach to behavior in Model B" leads to the quantities demanded and supplied, the D_j and the S_j, being relative quantities demanded and relative quantities supplied. This, in turn, results in the D_j and the S_j each always adding up to W which reflects the limited volume of resources of the system.

This is because the D_j and the S_j, in being relative quantities, will each adjust in a relative manner to always sum to W. Moreover, the D_j and the S_j depend only on the relative prices. Hence the quantities in Model B" are relative quantities; and these relative quantities depend only on the relative price.

We may also readily see that Model B" is characterized by long-run market processes that stem from the system's demand and supply functions.

Referring to the demand functions (7"), we find that since it is the relative quantities of commodities demanded that are determined in the system, the quantities demanded always sum to the overall output or income of the system, W.

Similarly, referring to the supply functions (8"), we find that since it is the relative quantities of commodities supplied that are determined in the system, the quantities supplied also always sum to the overall output or income of the system, W.

Consequently, as the relative prices change, an excess demand (supply) anywhere in the system is automatically matched by an equal excess supply (demand) elsewhere in the system. Hence overall excess demand (supply) is always zero.

This, of course, is a reflection of Model B being characterized by long-run market processes, processes that stem from the behavioral character of the system as reflected in the system's demand and supply functions. Whereas Model A's long-run market processes owe their existence to Say's Law.

6.6 The Behavioral Character Of The Revised Classical System

We shall now discuss how the new aspect to behavior that we bring into our new systems is formally incorporated into the systems. Model B" is shown below, this being the more detailed form of Model B:

Model B"

7". $\quad D_j = F'_j[W, f(z)]$

8". $\quad S_j = G'_j[W, g(z)]$

9". $\quad E'_j[W, f(z) - g(z) = 0] = 0$

The new aspect to behavior that we bring into our new systems is reflected in us taking individuals and firms to be aware that their resources are limited and hence they act in light of this awareness.

There are two facets to this aspect to behavior: First, individuals and firms are taken to be aware that their resources are limited. Second, this means that they act in light of this awareness.

Clearly, we can capture how individuals and firms are aware that their resources are limited only if these resources appear within their behavioral functions and hence within their demand and supply functions.

This is the case with Model B" since the system's limited resources, which are represented by W, appear explicitly within the system's demand and supply functions. This is how we capture in Model B" that individuals and firms are aware that their resources are limited.

Moreover, not only are individuals and firms made aware in Model B", in the manner discussed, that their resources are limited. They also act in light of this awareness.

This, of course, is ensured by functions $f(z)$ and $g(z)$ also appearing within the demand and supply functions of Model B". Functions $f(z)$ and $g(z)$ then operate on W to determine the D_j and the S_j.

This also accounts for the variable W being drawn into the behavioral content of Model B". This is because functions $f(z)$ and $g(z)$ determine the D_j and the S_j by operating on W; and since functions $f(z)$ and $g(z)$ are within the behavioral content of the system, so also is W.

This reflects how W, the overall output or income of Model B", becomes the system's internal budget constraint. Hence we have captured through the demand and supply functions of Model B", the aspect to the behavior of individuals and firms that is missing from the orthodox systems.

6.7 Why There Is A Correct Form Of Say's Law In The Revised Classical System

Say's Law, whether in its incorrect form as in Model A, or in its correct form as in Model B", always carries with it the meaning of a budget constraint in always implying that the resources of a system are limited.

Hence the Law always implies the variable W which, while reflecting the overall output or income of both Model A and Model B", also reflects the limited resources or budget constraint of the systems.

Model A's functions, however, cause the system to be initially inconsistent in a mathematical sense; and economists then impose the Law on the system to make it consistent. This does not suppress the meaning of the Law as a budget constraint in not suppressing how the Law always implies the variable W.

However, the Law is given an external character in Model A. This is because it is imposed on Model A from outside the system to make the system consistent. This means that W, in being implied by the Law, cannot possibly enter the behavioral content of Model A with W hence being put outside the behavioral content of the system.

Consequently, the Law in Model A is made to act as a budget constraint that is imposed on the system from outside the system. Let us now consider Model B". This system, as we discussed in Section 6.4, is automatically consistent in a mathematical sense. As a result, we do not need to impose the Law from the outside on Model B" to make the latter system consistent as has to be done in the case of Model A.

This removes W from outside the behavioral content of Model A; and this causes W to enter the behavioral content of Model B" as an internal budget constraint to hence enter the latter system's demand and supply functions.

This reflects how we internalize in Model B", the external budget constraint of Model A that is reflected in the latter system by the system's Say's Law.

This movement of W into the behavioral content of Model B", in turn, reflects how individuals and firms, through W, are made aware in Model B" that their resources are limited. Functions $f(z)$ and $g(z)$ then reflect how they act in light of this awareness. This, to review, is through functions $f(z)$ and $g(z)$ operating on W to determine the D_j and the S_j.

There was, however, an important precondition for the Law to enter the behavioral content of Model B" in the form of the variable W. This is because this required that the Law in Model B be rid of invalid elements and an invalid role that characterize Model A's form of the Law.

These invalid elements are the aggregate demand and supply variables that appear in the Say's Law identity, that is, in the identity $ad \equiv as$ that characterizes Model A. These aggregate demand and supply variables are then used to eliminate a surplus equation from Model A.

However, these variables, and hence their use to eliminate a surplus equation from Model A are invalid because they arise on account of the inconsistency in Model A. This led to Model A being initially inconsistent in a mathematical sense.

Then the aggregate demand and supply variables are created by economists describing W, now taken as reflecting the overall output or income of the system, alternately as aggregate demand and aggregate supply.

These aggregate demand and supply variables are then used to eliminate the surplus equation from Model A to make the system mathematically consistent; since it is only on account of these variables that we could have used the Law to rid Model A of a surplus equation.

However, we have resolved the inconsistency of Model A through Model B'' and we found that the latter system is automatically consistent in a mathematical sense. Hence we did not have to create the aggregate demand and supply variables in Model B'' and use them to eliminate a surplus equation from the system.

Consequently, we have rid the Say's Law in Model B'' of the invalid aggregate demand and supply variables of Model A's Say's Law as well as of the invalid role given to these variables in Model A of eliminating a surplus equation from the latter system.

This ridding of the Law of these invalid elements and role was, however, only possible because W entered the behavioral content of Model B''; since these invalid elements and role could only have characterized the Law in Model A because the Law exists outside Model A's behavioral content.

Hence it is through our bringing W into the behavioral content of Model B'' that we rid the Law in this system of the invalid elements and role that characterize Model A's form of the Law. This explains why a correct form of the Law enters Model B''.

Clearly, it would be expected that W, in entering the behavioral content of Model B, would result in the Law in the system being rid of the invalid elements and role that characterize Model A's form of the Law.

This is because Model B reflects how individuals and firms are aware that their resources are limited and hence they act in light of this awareness. Moreover, they are made aware that their resources are limited by W entering the behavioral content of the system as illustrated by Model B''.

This required that a true indication of their resources, meaning W, enter the system's behavioral content; since only through this variable could individuals and firms be made truly aware that their resources are limited. This, in turn, required that W be removed from the Say's Law identity, that is, from the identity $ad \equiv as$ and put into the behavioral content of Model B.

This was accomplished through our collapsing the aggregate demand and supply variables in the Say's Law identity into the single variable W that then entered into Model B's demand and supply functions.

We thereby brought a correct form of the Law into Model B, as will be confirmed in Chapter 9, to explain how through this system, we resolve the issues of the Law and the restriction of the classical system to long-run states. Whereas, as we shall now discuss, an incorrect form of the Law enters Model A and restricts the system to long-run states.

6.8 Why There Is An Incorrect Form Of Say's Law In The Orthodox Classical System

We have seen that the variable W appears explicitly within the behavioral content of Model B" and reflects how individuals and firms in the system are made aware that their resources are limited. This variable, in reflecting the limited resources of individuals and firms is already, of course, within the behavioral content of both Model A and Model B".

This is because W appears as an independent variable in the demand and supply functions of both Model A and Model B". Hence it influences the demands and supplies of individuals and firms in both systems.

However, while influencing the demands and supplies of Model A, W does not reflect in this latter system how individuals and firms are aware that their resources are limited. This is because Model A is not characterized by the interior functions $f(z)$ and $g(z)$ of Model B".

These latter functions, as we have seen, capture in Model B", the aspect to the behavior of individuals and firms reflected in us taking them to be aware that their resources are limited and hence they act in light of this awareness.

This meant that to capture such behavior, there must be a means whereby individuals and firms are made aware that their resources are limited; and as we have also shown, functions $f(z)$ and $g(z)$ themselves bring W into Model B" in a manner that makes individuals and firms aware that their resources are limited. This, as we discussed earlier, is through these functions bringing W into the system's behavioral content.

Moreover, functions $f(z)$ and $g(z)$ also reflect how individuals and firms act in light of this awareness. This is through these functions operating on W to determine the quantities demanded and supplied.

However, since Model A lacks functions $f(z)$ and $g(z)$ of Model B", the need to make individuals and firms aware that their resources are limited, as required by functions $f(z)$ and $g(z)$ of Model B", is suppressed in Model A.

Hence there was also no need to bring W into the behavioral content of Model A in the manner that is required in Model B" on account of functions $f(z)$ and $g(z)$ of the latter system. We may now readily see why there is an incorrect form of Say's Law in Model A and why this incorrect Law restricts the system to long-run states.

Although the need to bring W into the behavioral content of Model A is suppressed by the system's functions, this variable must yet be brought into the system. This is because it reflects the limited resources of the system.

As well, Model A's very same functions that suppressed the need to put W into the system's behavioral content, bring W into the system, but incorrectly. This, as we shall now discuss, explains why the hidden inconsistency we have uncovered entered Model A as well as explaining why there is an incorrect form of Say's Law in the system.

Model A's functions lead to the system being initially inconsistent in a mathematical sense. Then Say's Law is imposed on the system from the outside to make it mathematically consistent. Hence clearly, the Law cannot possibly bring W into the behavioral content of Model A.

This means that while Say's Law does bring W into Model A, this variable is left outside the behavioral content of the system. Hence while Say's Law ensures that Model A is consistent with limited resources, this is ensured by Say's Law being imposed on the system from the outside to make the system mathematically consistent.

This brings inconsistency into Model A; since the system should be made consistent with limited resources by the behavior or economic rationale of the system as in Model B. Moreover, the inconsistency of Model A is reflected in consistency of the system with limited resources being ensured by the system being made mathematically consistent; and Say's Law is the means whereby the system is made mathematically consistent.

Clearly, this explains why an incorrect form of the Law enters Model A. Hence Model A's incorrect form of Say's Law enters the system as a result of the hidden inconsistency we have uncovered in the system.

This incorrect form of the Law, in turn, restricts Model A to long-run states. As a result, Model B, in being rid of this inconsistency, and hence of Model A's incorrect form of Say's Law, is not restricted to long-run states.

This means that Model B will move to short-run states as behavior changes, a reflection of the system, while being a microeconomic system, yet having a macroeconomic character.

6.9 There Is A More General Approach To Rational Behavior In The New Systems

We discussed in Chapter 2.3, the new aspect to the behavior of individuals and firms that we bring into our new systems, an aspect to behavior that is missing from orthodox systems; and we shall now discuss how this behavior translates into an aspect to rational behavior that is hence also missing from orthodox systems.

Below are the demand and supply functions of Model B":

7". $\quad D_j \equiv F'_j [W, f(z)]$

8". $\quad S_j \equiv G'_j [W, g(z)]$

These functions reflect a more general approach to rational behavior compared to the orthodox functions. This is because unlike Model A's functions, the functions of Model B" imply that individuals and firms determine the quantities of commodities they demand and supply in the knowledge or awareness that their resources are limited.

Both functions (7") and (8") of Model B" contain the variable W that reflects the limited resources or budget constraint of individuals and firms.

Next, the quantities demanded and supplied, the D_j and the S_j, can only be determined by functions $f(z)$ and $g(z)$ operating respectively on the variable W which, to review, represents the limited resources or budget constraint of individuals and firms.

This reflects how individuals and firms in Model B", in determining the quantities they demand and supply, are necessarily aware of their limited resources or budget constraint as reflected in the variable W.

This endows the W in Model B" with utility; since there is utility to individuals and firms of a variable, which is W, that reflects their limited resources or budget constraint. This, however, is not the case with Model A.

This is because the budget constraint W of Model A is imposed on the system from outside the system by Say's Law.

Hence W is outside the behavioral content of the system. As a result, the W in Model A cannot possibly reflect how individuals and firms in the system are aware that their resources are limited. Consequently, the W in Model A is not endowed with utility.

Whereas W is within the demand and supply functions of Model B" where, as discussed, it reflects how individuals and firms are aware of their limited resources or budget constraint; and this endows the W in Model B" with utility. Hence Model B" is characterized by a more general approach to rational behavior compared to Model A.

We may best describe this new approach to rational behavior as reflecting how individuals and firms in Model B, acting rationally, determine their commodity demands and supplies in the knowledge or awareness that their resources are limited. Whereas this is not the case in orthodox systems such as Model A.

There are many consequences of this new approach to the rational behavior of individuals and firms. Most generally, however, it accounts for us resolving the inconsistency of Model A through Model B". Moreover, as will now be discussed, it is the underlying reason why we resolved the issue of Say's Law.

6.10 The Rational Behavior Of Model B Resolves The Issue Of Say's Law

We discussed in Sections 6.7 and 6.8 how the issue of Say's Law was resolved through Model B. However, we shall now go further into the behavioral rationale of the system that accounts for this. This stems from the rational behavior we have described that characterizes Model B.

To review, we derived the variable W by collapsing the aggregate demand and supply variables in the Say's Law identity of Model A into the single variable W. This variable reflects Model A's overall output or income although we had to elicit it from the system in the manner described.

Next, Model A is initially inconsistent in a mathematical sense. Then Say's Law is imposed on the system to eliminate a surplus equation to make it mathematically consistent. This meant that the variable W, in being implied by the Law, is also imposed on Model A from outside the system.

Hence this variable exists outside the behavioral content of Model A; and this is because the system lacks the rational behavior that characterizes Model B. This rational behavior, to review, reflects how individuals and firms, acting rationally, determine their demands and supplies in the knowledge or awareness that their resources are limited.

This gives utility to individuals and firms of a variable that reflects their limited resources or budget constraint; and this variable is W. This accounts for the W moving from outside the behavioral content of Model A into the behavioral content of Model B.

This results in the W in Model B also taking on the meaning of a budget constraint that provides the basis for the maximization behavior of individuals and firms.

This is reflected in Model B's interior functions, functions $f(z)$ and $g(z)$, operating respectively on W to determine the quantities of commodities demanded and supplied. Hence although we leave the maximizing behavior of individuals and firms implicit in our analysis, we must assume that these quantities result from the maximizing behavior of the individual and the firm.

We may now readily see how the approach to rational behavior of Model B accounts for us resolving the issue of Say's Law. As was discussed in Section 6.7 above, the variable W in Model B is the means whereby individuals and firms are made aware that their resources are limited.

Moreover, this variable was brought into the behavioral content of Model B on account of the rational behavior of individuals and firms. However, this variable is implicit in Model A's Say's Law. Hence it had to be removed from this Say's Law in order to enter the behavioral content of Model B.

This, of course, was accomplished by our collapsing the aggregate demand and supply variables in the Say's Law identity into the single variable W. Hence it is the rational behavior of Model B that required that W be removed from the Say's Law of Model A in order that it may enter the behavioral content of Model B.

Moreover, once we collapsed the Law to form the variable W, the Law could not now be used to ensure mathematical consistency of Model A. However, this is where the new approach to behavior in Model B came into the picture.

As we discussed in Section 6.4 of the chapter, Model B is automatically consistent in a mathematical sense. Hence we did not need Say's Law to make the system mathematically consistent; and this rid Model B of Model A's incorrect form of the Law.

Hence since it is the behavior underlying Model B that accounts for the system being automatically consistent in a mathematical sense, it is this behavior that resolved the issue of Say's Law. Hence by the same token, it is because Model A lacks the behavior that characterizes Model B, that Model A reflects an incorrect form of the Law.

6.11 Remarks On The Revised Classical System

We have now set out our revised classical system using two forms of the system, Model B and Model B''. However, since the systems are interchangeable, we shall frequently drop the superscript from Model B''.

Overall, however, Model B, in being a less detailed form of our new system, is best suited for describing the general character of the system and will be used primarily for this purpose in later chapters of the book. However, Model B'' allowed us to bring out the detailed behavioral character of the system; and this required focusing on a special role of the variable W.

This variable reflects the limited resources or budget constraint of individuals and firms; and as such, it appears as an independent variable in the demand and supply functions of Model B. Hence W influences the demands and supplies in the system. However, we do not focus on this role of W.

Instead, we are mainly concerned with the role that W plays as a budget constraint. This is in the sense that the quantities demanded (supplied) in our new systems must each necessarily sum to W.

Next, to assist us in explaining this role in Model B, we brought W in its role as a budget constraint, which is implicit in Model B, explicitly into the demand and supply functions of Model B''. This allowed us, as we saw in the chapter, to explain in detail the behavioral character of Model B and how this differs from that of Model A.

Hence while we shall frequently refer to the variable W later in the book, we shall usually be referring to the role this variable plays as reflecting the limited resources or budget constraint of Model B and not to the other role we have described that this variable also plays in the system.

6.12 Summary

We developed our new type of demand and supply functions in this chapter, functions that form the basis for our revised classical system, Model B. These new functions, unlike the orthodox-type functions such as characterize Model A, correctly reflect economic behavior in reflecting behavior that is consistent with limitation in resources. Hence through Model B, we resolved the hidden inconsistency of Model A.

Moreover, as discussed in Section 6.7, Model B reflects a correct form of Say's Law, a form of the Law that cannot restrict the system to long-run states. Whereas there is an incorrect form of the Law in Model A, see Section 6.8, a form of the Law that restricts this latter system to long-run states.

Hence Model B, although being a microeconomic system, yet has a macroeconomic character, in that it can move to alternative states as behavior changes. This is because it is rid of the incorrect form of Say's Law of Model A that restricts the latter system to long-run states, which suppresses the system's macroeconomic character.

Finally, we discussed how our new systems reflect an aspect to rational behavior that is missing from orthodox systems and how this behavior accounts for us resolving the issue of Say's Law.

Chapter 7

Generality Of The Revised Classical System

7.1 Introduction

We have now set out the inconsistency we have uncovered in the orthodox classical system, Model A. Moreover, we have resolved this inconsistency through Model B; and in the following chapter, we shall review in an overall way how this inconsistency has been resolved.

However, in this chapter, we shall focus on bringing out the more detailed aspects of the rationale of Model B. This is to establish how through the latter system, we provide the basis to integrate microeconomic and macroeconomic systems.

7.2 Integrating Microeconomic And Macroeconomic Systems

We show Model B" below, this being the more detailed form of Model B that was set out in Chapter 6:

Model B"

7".	$D_j = F'_j[W, f(z)]$
8".	$S_j = G'_j[W, g(z)]$
9".	$E'_j[W, f(z) - g(z) = 0] = 0$

Model B" is a wholly microeconomic system. This is because the variable W reflects the limited resources or budget constraint of individuals and firms. Functions $f(z)$ and $g(z)$ then operate respectively on W to determine the individual quantities of commodities demanded and supplied, the D_j and S_j.

These quantities then enter the markets of the system, reflecting how the system how a microeconomic character. Yet the system also has a macroeconomic character which is reflected in it being characterized by a behaviorally-determined overall output; since W not only reflects the system's limited resources but also the overall output or income of the system. Hence Model B" has a dual microeconomic-macroeconomic character; and this is due to the rational behavior in the system.

Let us assume that Model B" reaches an initial equilibrium with a set of individual quantities being determined, these individual quantities of commodities constituting the resources of individuals and firms.

Next, as was discussed in Chapter 6.9, the rational behavior of Model B" implies that individuals and firms determine their demands and supplies in the knowledge or awareness that their resources are limited.

This gives utility to a variable that reflects their overall resources; and this results in the individual quantities that are determined in Model B" being transformed by the system's rational behavior into the aggregative variable W that reflects their overall resources.

This variable reflects a summation of the individual quantities of commodities determined in the system; and this W then enters the system's demand and supply functions as a budget constraint.

Clearly, the variable W also reflects the overall output of the system in being a summation of the individual quantities that are determined in the system. Next, these individual quantities, as we discussed, are determined by the system's microeconomic market processes.

Hence there is a behaviorally-determined overall output or income variable W in Model B" which gives the system a macroeconomic character. However, the system's macroeconomic character is consistent with the system being a microeconomic system; since the overall output or income variable W of Model B" is determined by or has its origin in the system's microeconomics.

This, to review, is because W is a summation of the individual quantities of commodities that are determined by the system's microeconomic market processes.

We have been considering Model B" as it describes an initial equilibrium. Let us, however, now discuss how the system moves among various equilibria; and we begin by assuming that the system is characterized by the W that has been determined, in the manner described, in the system's initial equilibrium.

Functions $f(z)$ and $g(z)$ then operate on this W to determine individual quantities of commodities demanded and supplied that enter the markets of the system. We next assume that a further equilibrium is reached where another set of individual quantities of commodities is determined. These quantities again constitute the resources of individuals and firms.

Then the rational behavior of individuals and firms transforms these individual quantities into a new variable W that enters the system as a new budget constraint. Moreover, this W again reflects the overall output of the system in that it is a summation of the individual quantities that are determined in the system.

As a result, we may look on Model B'' as moving through a series of microeconomic equilibria that are determined by the operation of the system's microeconomic market processes.

However, in each of these microeconomic equilibria, a macroeconomic variable W that simultaneously reflects the overall output or income of the system as well as the system's budget constraint, arises. This is on account of the rational behavior of individuals and firms.

Hence W is behaviorally determined which gives the system a macroeconomic character. However, it is determined by the operation of the system's microeconomic market processes and hence by the behavior of the individual and the firm.

Consequently, while Model B'' has a macroeconomic character, this macroeconomic character arises out of the system's microeconomics and hence out of the behavior of the individual and the firm. This reflects how through Model B, we integrate microeconomic and macroeconomic systems.

7.3 Generality Of The Revised Classical System

Model B has a macroeconomic character in that it is characterized by a behaviorally-determined macroeconomic variable W that simultaneously reflects both the overall output and budget constraint of the system.

Moreover, as we have discussed, the variable W arises in Model B on account of the rational behavior of individuals and firms and hence out of the microeconomics of the system. There are, in turn, two key consequences of this which will allow us to show that Model B has a more general character than both Model A and the Keynesian system.

First, the variable W in Model B, in arising out of the internal microeconomics of the system, cannot possibly restrict the system to any specific state. Hence Model B will move to alternative states as behavior changes. This confirms that the system has a macroeconomic character.

Second, the variable W of Model B, as discussed, arises out of the internal microeconomics of the system. Hence it also cannot possibly suppress or restrict the microeconomics of the system. We are now in a position to compare Model B with Model A and the Keynesian system.

To assist us in comparing Model A, Model B and the Keynesian system, we denoted the overall output or income of all of these systems by the variable W. However, the different forms of behavior in the systems affect the exact nature of W in each of the systems.

As we have discussed, the W of Model B cannot possibly restrict the system to any particular state and, as well, it cannot possibly restrict the microeconomic character of the system. Let us now consider Model A.

The overall output variable W of this system is imposed on the system from outside the system by Say's Law which is used to make the system mathematically consistent. This restricts Model A to long-run states. Let us now consider the Keynesian system.

This system's overall output variable W directly enters the market processes of the system, to be determined by aggregate demand and supply functions. However, these functions suppress or abstract from the microeconomics of the real part of the system.

Model B's overall output variable W, however, as we have discussed, cannot possibly restrict the system to any particular state and, as well, it cannot possibly restrict the system's microeconomics. Consequently, Model B has a more general character compared to both the classical system, Model A, and the Keynesian system.

7.4 The Macroeconomic Character Of Model B

Say's Law is represented in the literature by the identity $ad \equiv as$; and we shall now take the Law as indeed a true identity. This means, as we did in Chapter 5.4, that we may collapse the aggregate demand and supply variables in the Say's Law identity to form the variable W.

This variable, to review, represents the overall output of Model A, a long-run output in the case of this system; and as well, W also reflects the limited resources or budget constraint of the system.

Next, Model A is initially inconsistent in a mathematical sense. Then Say's Law in the form of the identity $ad \equiv as$ is imposed on the system to eliminate a surplus equation to make the system mathematically consistent.

Hence the identity $ad \equiv as$ is created by economists describing W alternately as aggregate demand and aggregate supply. Then this identity is imposed on Model A to eliminate a surplus equation to make the system mathematically consistent.

This means that the identity $ad \equiv as$ in Model A is an incorrect form of Say's Law since it is given a substantive role in Model A of making the system mathematically consistent. However, in being a true identity, it should not be given such a role. This accounts for there being an incorrect form of the Law in Model A, a form of the Law that restricts the system to long-run states. This has been resolved by the functions of Model B".

These brought into the latter system, an aspect to the behavior of individuals and firms that is missing from Model A. This, to review, is the aspect to behavior that ensures that a system is consistent with limitation in resources.

This, as we showed in Chapter 6.4 through Model B, resulted in Model B" being automatically consistent in a mathematical sense. As a result, we did not need the Say's Law identity to make Model B" mathematically consistent, which rid the latter system of Model A's incorrect form of Say's Law.

Moreover, we were able to show exactly how this occurred by examining the behavioral character of Model B".

Functions $f(z)$ and $g(z)$ of Model B", which reflect the new aspect to behavior we brought into the system, must be accompanied by the variable W; since only by operating on W can functions $f(z)$ and $g(z)$ determine the quantities of commodities demanded and supplied in the system.

Hence since functions $f(z)$ and $g(z)$ are in the behavioral content of Model B", so also is the variable W. This, as was discussed in Chapter 6.7, rid Say's Law of invalid elements. These are the aggregate demand and supply variables in the Say's Law identity $ad \equiv as$ of Model A.

As a result, we also rid Model B" of the invalid use of these variables in Model A to eliminate a surplus equation from the latter system. Hence a true or correct form of the Law entered Model B", meaning a form of the Law that is rid of the invalid elements and role that characterize the Law in Model A.

Consequently, Model B" is rid of Model A's incorrect form of Say's Law that restricts the latter system to long-run states. This means that Model B" is not restricted by the Law to long-run states, hence the system will move to short-run states were behavior to change to short-run behavior.

As a result, Model B" has a macroeconomic character yet the system is a microeconomic system in being based wholly on the behavior of the individual and the firm.

7.5 Further Remarks On The Macroeconomic Character Of Model B

We have, through resolving the hidden inconsistency of Model A, brought a correct form of Say's Law into Model B". This resulted in the overall output variable W being moved from outside the behavioral content of Model A, where it had been put by Say's Law, into the behavioral content of Model B". This transforms the meaning of W in the latter system.

Clearly, W, in being outside the behavioral content of Model A, is necessarily non-behavioral in character hence it cannot possibly be influenced by the behavior or market processes of the system.

This restricts W to reflecting a non-behaviorally determined long-run overall output which restricts Model A to long-run states. However, W, in being brought into the behavioral content of Model B", is given a behavioral character.

This is because W is transformed in Model B" from reflecting a long-run output that is non-behavioral in character in Model A, to become a long-run output that is behaviorally determined in Model B"; since W is now determined in Model B" by the behavior of the system as reflected in the operation of the system's market processes.

Moreover, unlike the Keynesian system, the W of Model B", as discussed in Section 7.2, is determined by microeconomic market processes. This is because the variable W enters the demand and supply functions of Model B as a budget constraint.

Functions $f(z)$ and $g(z)$ then operate on W to determine the individual quantities of commodities demanded and supplied that enter the markets of the system. Hence Model B" is a microeconomic system. Yet the system also has a macroeconomic character.

This is because the individual quantities of commodities that are determined in the system are transformed by the rational behavior of individuals and firms, back into an overall output or income variable W. This W then re-enters the system's demand and supply functions as a budget constraint. Consequently, overall output or income W is behaviorally determined in Model B" but by microeconomic market processes.

Whereas the overall output or income of the Keynesian system is determined by aggregate demand and supply functions; but these functions suppress or abstract from the microeconomics of the real part of the Keynesian system.

Hence both Model B" and the Keynesian system have a macroeconomic character reflected in both systems having a behaviorally-determined overall output or income variable. Yet Model B is a wholly microeconomic system whereas the microeconomics of the real part of the Keynesian system is suppressed.

7.6 Rational Behavior Gives Model B A Simultaneous Microeconomic-Macroeconomic Character

Keynes' key contribution lies in forming his macroeconomic system that describes short-run states that are characterized by general unemployment. However, the macroeconomic character of the Keynesian system comes largely at the expense of the system's microeconomics. This may be seen by discussing the Keynesian system against the backdrop of Model B.

This latter system, as we have shown, is rid of the incorrect form of Say's Law that restricts Model A to long-run states. As a result, Model B can move to short-run states were behavior to change to short-run behavior, the system hence having a macroeconomic character.

Yet this is consistent with the system being a wholly microeconomic system. This is on account of the rational behavior in the system.

To review, rational behavior in Model B is reflected in individuals and firms determining their commodity demands and supplies in the knowledge or awareness that their resources are limited; and this gives utility to a variable that reflects the limited resources or budget constraint of individuals and firms.

This, in turn, gives rise to an aggregative or macroeconomic variable W that not only reflects the overall output or income of Model B. As well, this W also simultaneously reflects the system's limited resources or budget constraint.

Moreover, this W of Model B is consistent with the system having a microeconomic character. This is because W enters Model B as a budget constraint resulting in it entering the system's demand and supply functions.

Next, the interior functions $f(z)$ and $g(z)$ of Model B operate on W to determine the individual quantities of commodities demanded and supplied. These quantities then enter the markets of the system, reflecting how Model B has a microeconomic character. Hence the macroeconomic variable W of Model B is consistent with the system having a microeconomic character.

Whereas the Keynesian W abstracts from or suppresses the microeconomics of the real part of the Keynesian system. As a result, the individual quantities of commodities and the commodity relative prices are suppressed in the system.

Clearly, we have, through our new approach to price systems, broken down a barrier between microeconomic and macroeconomic systems.

Model B and the Keynesian system both have a behaviorally-determined overall output variable W reflecting how both systems have a macroeconomic character. However, the W in Model B is not itself a market-determined variable as in the Keynesian system.

Hence aggregate demand and supply functions such as characterize the Keynesian system, and which determine the W in the latter system, do not exist in Model B.

This is because what are determined by market processes in Model B are individual quantities of commodities, these being determined by microeconomic market processes. These individual quantities of commodities are then transformed by rational behavior into the aggregative or macroeconomic variable W.

This W then enters Model B" as an income or budget constraint rather than being itself a market-determined variable as in the Keynesian system. Functions $f(z)$ and $g(z)$ of Model B" then operate on this budget constraint to determine the individual quantities of commodities demanded and supplied, a reflection of the system's microeconomic character.

7.7 Why The Keynesian System Does Not Have A Satisfactory Microeconomic Basis

Keynes' macroeconomic system is characterized by a behaviorally determined overall output that we denoted by W; and this overall flow of output or income must necessarily accrue to individuals and firms to become their limited resources or budget constraint.

However, there is no means in the Keynesian system to capture how the overall output or income variable W becomes the budget or income constraint of individuals and firms. This is because the Keynesian system lacks the aspect to behavior that we brought into Model B.

This aspect to behavior, to review, reflects how we take individuals and firms to be aware that their resources are limited and hence they act in light of this awareness. Moreover, there has to be some means whereby individuals and firms are made aware that their resources, as reflected in the overall output variable W, are limited; and this is the case with Model B.

This is through overall output or income W being brought as a budget or income constraint into the behavioral content of Model B, that is, into the system's overall demand and supply functions, by the interior functions $f(z)$ and $g(z)$.

This reflected how individuals and firms in Model B are made aware that their resources, as reflected in W, are limited. Next, they act in light of this awareness. This is through the same functions $f(z)$ and $g(z)$ of Model B operating on W to determine the individual quantities of commodities demanded and supplied, reflecting how Model B has a microeconomic character.

However, the microeconomic processes that characterize Model B are missing from the Keynesian system. This is because the system lacks the aspect to behavior we brought into Model B in lacking functions of the type of $f(z)$ and $g(z)$ that characterize Model B.

This, to review, is the aspect to behavior reflected in us taking individuals and firms to be aware that their resources are limited and hence they act in light of this awareness.

Consequently, the overall output or income variable W is not brought as an income or budget constraint of relevance to microeconomics into the behavioral content of the Keynesian system as is the case with Model B. Hence the microeconomic market processes of Model B that determine individual quantities of commodities and the commodity relative prices are missing from the Keynesian system.

This, moreover, is reflected in the overall output of the Keynesian system, W, rather than individual quantities of commodities demanded and supplied, entering the market processes of the Keynesian system.

Overall output W is then determined by Keynes' aggregate demand and supply functions. However, these functions suppress the microeconomics of the real part of the Keynesian system. Whereas individual quantities of commodities demanded and supplied enter the markets of Model B, reflecting how the system has a satisfactory microeconomic character.

7.8 Remarks On The New Long And Short-Run Systems

We have discussed how short-run or macroeconomic systems emerge out of our revised classical system, Model B, which is a long-run system. However, we do not develop short-run systems in detail in this book.

Nonetheless, we shall deal with short-run or macroeconomic systems but only by focusing on the general economic logic of the systems rather than on the specific forms of behavior of individual systems; and we shall base our analyses of the general economic logic of our short-run systems on the general economic logic of the long-run Model B.

This is because the general economic logic of the latter system is also relevant to short-run systems.

Model B, to review, reflects an aspect to the behavior of individuals and firms that is missing from Model A. This is the aspect to behavior reflected in us taking individuals and firms to be aware that their resources are limited and hence they act in light of this awareness.

This leads to a more general approach to rational behavior that was discussed in Chapter 6.9. This rational behavior, to review, is reflected in individuals and firms, acting rationally, determining their demands and supplies in the knowledge or awareness that their resources are limited.

Clearly, although short-run or macroeconomic systems will differ in many respects from the long-run Model B, this approach to rational behavior of Model B also necessarily applies to short-run systems. In fact, it applies to price systems in general.

There is a further basic similarity between Model B and short-run systems that we have already brought out but which will be more fully covered in Chapter 10.

We have shown in Chapter 5 that the limited resources or the budget constraint of Model B is reflected in the overall output of the system. Moreover, we shall discuss in Chapter 10 how the system's overall output, and hence the system's budget constraint, is behaviorally determined.

This is because overall output, and hence the system's budget constraint, is determined by the behavior in the system as reflected in the operation of the system's market equilibrating processes.

Hence Model B is subject to a budget constraint that is determined internally in the system by the system's behavior or market processes; and as will also be discussed in Chapter 10, this is a property that applies not only to Model B but also to macroeconomic or short-run systems that are based on the similar approach as Model B.

7.9 Summary

We set out earlier the inconsistency we have uncovered in the orthodox classical system, Model A. Moreover, we also set out Model B in the preceding chapter, a system through which we resolve Model A's inconsistency; and we shall review in an overall way in the following chapter how this inconsistency has been resolved. However, in this chapter, we set out in detail the rationale of Model B.

To review, we have rid Model B of an incorrect form of Say's Law that restricts Model A to long-run states. As a result, Model B is not necessarily restricted to long-run states hence the system will move to short-run states were behavior to change.

This gives Model B a macroeconomic character even though the system is a microeconomic system in being based wholly on the behavior of the individual and the firm. Hence Model B is more general that the orthodox classical system, Model A; since the macroeconomic character of the latter system is suppressed.

Moreover, Model B is also more general than the Keynesian system. This is because while both systems have a macroeconomic character, Model B is a wholly microeconomic system. Whereas the microeconomics of the real part of the Keynesian system is suppressed.

Finally, we discussed how the general logic of the long-run or microeconomic Model B" also extends, in principle, to short-run or macroeconomic systems.

Chapter 8

Resolving The Inconsistency In The Classical System

8.1 Introduction

Model A, the orthodox classical system, is initially inconsistent in an economic sense. This is because the behavior in the system, and hence the system's functions, do not ensure that the system is consistent with limitation in resources. However, we resolved this inconsistency through Model B.

This was done by basing the latter system on our relative demand and supply functions. These new functions ensure that Model B is consistent with limitation in resources. As a result, we resolved Model A's economic inconsistency through Model B.

Moreover, we thereby also resolved, through Model B, the mathematical reflection in Model A of the latter system's economic inconsistency. This is because Model B, unlike Model A, is automatically consistent in a mathematical sense.

We shall also review in the chapter how we have resolved the hidden inconsistency of Model A, and similar orthodox systems, through generalizing the orthodox approach to microeconomics.

Consequently, while our new systems have a macroeconomic character, this macroeconomic character stems from our more general approach to microeconomics underlying the systems. Finally, we shall provide an overview of our new approach to price systems.

8.2 Resolving Model A's Economic Inconsistency

Model A is subject to a hidden economic inconsistency because consistency of the system with limitation in resources is not correctly ensured.

Consistency with limitation in resources is a condition for economic consistency of a system. As a result, it should be ensured by the system's behavior or economic rationale and hence by the system's demand and supply functions. However, Model A's functions do not ensure that the system is consistent with limitation in resources. Instead, consistency with limited resources is ensured in Model A as a consequence of the system being made mathematically consistent by Say's Law.

Hence a condition for economic consistency of Model A, namely, consistency with limited resources, is ensured by the system being made mathematically consistent rather than by the system's behavior or economic rationale. This inconsistency of Model A, however, has been resolved through Model B.

This is because Model B's demand and supply functions reflect an aspect to the behavior of individuals and firms that is missing from the orthodox systems. This is the aspect to behavior that ensures that price systems are consistent with limitation in resources.

This results in Model B's functions determining relative quantities of commodities demanded (supplied). Hence these quantities, in being relative quantities, will adjust in a relative manner so that they always sum to the total of Model B's given resources.

As a result, consistency with limited resources is correctly ensured in Model B in being ensured by the system's behavior or economic rationale, to resolve the hidden economic inconsistency of Model A.

8.3 Resolving The Mathematical Reflection Of Model A's Economic Inconsistency

We showed in Chapter 6.4 that Model B is automatically consistent in a mathematical sense. This results from consistency of the system's behavior or economic rationale.

This is because this economic rationale is reflected in the system's demand and supply functions; and these functions correctly reflect economic behavior in reflecting behavior that is consistent with limitation in resources.

This results in Model B's demand and supply functions automatically ensuring mathematical consistency of the system, since the functions lead to a number of independent equations that equals the number of unknowns in the system.

Hence mathematical consistency of Model B, as reflected in the system meeting the equation-counting rule, is a result of consistency of the system's general economic logic or rationale. This resolves the mathematical reflection of Model A's economic inconsistency.

This, to review, is reflected in mathematical consistency of Model A being given precedence over the system's behavior or economic rationale in ensuring that the system is consistent with limitation in resources. Whereas mathematical consistency of Model B is a consequence of the system's general economic consistency as reflected in consistency of the system with limitation in resources.

8.4 General Solution To The Inconsistency In The Classical System

Consistency in any field of study should be ensured by consistency of the substantive content of that field. Hence consistency of the general economic logic of price systems, meaning consistency of the systems with limited resources, should be ensured by the systems' behavior or economic rationale.

Instead, consistency of the general economic logic of orthodox price systems such as Model A, or consistency of the systems with limited resources, is ensured as a result of the systems being made mathematically consistent.

To review, Model A is made consistent by being made mathematically consistent. Next, mathematical consistency ensures consistency of the system's general logic; and this means that we may solve the system for its equilibrium quantities and prices.

However, we must, of course, also assume that the system is subject to limitation in resources. Hence the quantities that we solve for must conform to this. That is, the quantities demanded (supplied) that we solve for must each sum to the limited volume of resources underlying the system.

Next, since it is in making the system mathematically consistent that we can solve for these quantities, mathematical consistency ensures that the system is consistent with limitation in resources. That is, it ensures consistency of the system's general economic logic. This is how inconsistency enters Model A.

This is because consistency with limited resources, or consistency of a system's general economic logic, is a condition for economic consistency of the system. Hence it should be ensured by the behavior or economic rationale of the system.

Instead, consistency with limited resources is ensured in Model A, and similar orthodox systems, as a consequence of the systems being made mathematically consistent, to bring inconsistency into the systems. Whereas consistency of our new systems with limitation in resources is ensured by the systems' behavior or economic rationale.

This behavior was discussed in Chapter 2.3; and we capture this behavior through our new type of demand and supply functions, our relative demand and supply functions, that form the basis for Model B. Consequently, limitation in resources is ensured behaviorally in Model B rather than by the system being made mathematically consistent.

Nonetheless, mathematical consistency, of course, remains in the picture with respect to Model B but in quite a different way compared to Model A. This is because Model B's functions automatically also ensure that the system is consistent in a mathematical sense.

Hence mathematical consistency of Model B is a result of the system's general economic consistency. This reflects in mathematical terms how Model A's economic inconsistency has been resolved through Model B.

Clearly, this economic inconsistency has been resolved because Model B's demand and supply functions are based on a more general approach to the behavior of the individual and the firm compared to Model A's functions.

This is because Model B's functions, while being subject to the usual conditions or axioms for consistency and rationality of behavior, also reflect an aspect to behavior that is prior in importance compared to these conditions.[16]

This, to review, is the aspect to behavior reflected in our taking individuals and firms to be aware that their resources are limited and hence they act in light of this awareness. This is confirmed by Model B's functions ensuring that the system is consistent with limitation in resources.

Hence through Model B, we resolved Model A's economic inconsistency; and as well, we also resolved through Model B, how this inconsistency is reflected in Model A in mathematical terms.

8.5 Generalizing The Orthodox Microeconomic Analysis

Individuals and firms in orthodox microeconomic systems are conceived of as demanding and supplying goods to maximize their utility and profit subject to a budget constraint; and our new systems are consistent with this behavior but generalizes it. This

---

[16] On the conditions or axioms for consistency and rationality of behavior in price systems see, for example, Henderson and Quandt, *op. cit.*, Chs. 2 and 3 and Vickrey, *op. cit.*, Chs. 2 and 4.

is through our bringing an aspect to behavior that is missing from the orthodox microeconomics.

To review, functions $f(z)$ and $g(z)$ of Model B that are within the system's overall demand and supply functions, operate on the variable W to determine the quantities of commodities demanded and supplied.

Next, the variable W reflects the overall output of the system; but as discussed in Chapter 5, it also simultaneously reflects the limited resources or budget constraint of individuals and firms.

Hence taking it that individuals and firms in Model B maximize their utility and profit subject to a budget constraint, we must assume that the quantities determined in Model B by functions $f(z)$ and the $g(z)$ operating on W, are a consequence of this maximizing behavior.

Moreover, not only is Model B, albeit implicitly, consistent with the maximizing behavior of individuals and firms along the lines discussed. Model B's functions also reflect an aspect to the behavior of individuals and firms that is missing from the orthodox microeconomic analysis.

This is the aspect to behavior reflected in us taking individuals and firms to be aware that their resources are limited and hence they act in light of this awareness; and this behavior translated, as we discussed in Chapter 6.9, into an aspect to rational behavior that is hence also missing from the orthodox microeconomic analysis.

As a result, we have generalized the orthodox microeconomic analysis by incorporating into it, an aspect to the behavior of individuals and firms, and an associated aspect to rational behavior, that are is missing from the orthodox analysis.

This accounted for our new functions that characterize Model B, resolving the hidden inconsistency of Model A; and as well, it explains why our new systems, while being microeconomic systems, yet have a macroeconomic character.

This is because Model B's functions not only bring a more general approach to microeconomics into the system. The functions, as well, rid Model B of an incorrect form of Say's Law that characterizes Model A and which restricts the latter system to long-run states. Hence Model B is not restricted to long-run states which means that the system will move to short-run states were behavior to change to short-run behavior.

Consequently, Model B has a macroeconomic character; and this is due to the more general form of microeconomics on which we have based the system, an approach to microeconomics we arrived at through resolving the hidden inconsistency of Model A.

8.6 An Overview Of The New Approach To Price Systems

Price systems, of course, must be based on the economic behavior of individuals and firms, meaning behavior that is consistent with limitation in resources; and in this book, we have set out a way to impose a general condition on our new systems to ensure that the systems reflect this behavior, irrespective of the differing forms of behavior the system may reflect.

Price systems are based on demand and supply functions; and we found a new type of such functions, our relative demand and supply functions, that not only capture the different forms of behavior of individual or particular systems.

These functions, through their relative character, also become the means to impose a condition for general economic consistency on all systems that are based on these functions, irrespective of the differing forms of behavior of individual systems.

This is because these new functions automatically ensure that any system based on them is consistent with limitation in resources or a budget constraint; and this is ensured by the systems' behavior or economic rationale in being ensured by the systems' demand and supply functions.

Furthermore, these new functions also ensure that our new systems are consistent in a mathematical sense. Hence we do not have to impose mathematical consistency on these new systems. This is because mathematical consistency becomes a result or consequence of the general economic consistency of the systems as reflected in consistency of the systems with limited resources.

On the other hand, the orthodox-type functions of systems such as Model A do not ensure that the systems are consistent with limitation in resources.

This is because the functions do not reflect the aspect to behavior that we brought into our new functions. As a result, the orthodox-type functions, unlike our new type of functions, do not initially determine relative quantities. Instead, the functions initially determine absolute quantities.

This means that these absolute quantities must be transformed into relative quantities to make them always sum to the given volume of resources of the orthodox systems. Let us review how this was accomplished by first focusing on Model A.

Model A is initially inconsistent in a mathematical sense in that there is a surplus equation over the number of unknowns; and this is because the system's functions do not ensure consistency of the system with limited resources.

Next, the system is made mathematically consistent by an external budget constraint, which is Say's Law, being imposed on the system; and this, as was discussed in Chapter 5, ensures that the system is consistent with limitation in resources by transforming quantities into relative quantities.

However, an economic inconsistency remains in Model A but becomes reflected in the system in mathematical terms. This is in mathematical consistency being given precedence over economic consistency in ensuring that the system is consistent with limitation in resources.

Moreover, having to make Model A consistent in the manner described, that is, by imposing an external budget constraint on the system, restricts the system to a specific state, a long-run state in this instance.

This also is not only the case with Model A; since all systems based on the orthodox-type demand and supply functions, like those of Model A, are also made consistent by external elements, namely, budget constraints, being imposed on the systems.

These external budget constraints, however, restrict the orthodox systems to specific states, these being the states associated with the volume of resources imposed on the systems by these budget constraints. Consequently, the orthodox systems, in being restricted to specific states, are dichotomized.

However, through imposing our overall condition for general economic consistency on our new systems through the systems' demand and supply functions, these systems are all automatically made consistent in a mathematical sense.

Hence mathematical consistency is a consequence of the general economic consistency of the new systems, meaning consistency of the systems with limited resources. As a result, we avoid having to impose consistency with limited resources on our new systems through imposing external budget constraints on them, as has to be done with the orthodox systems.

As a result, we avoided the restriction of our new systems to specific states to also avoid the dichotomization of the systems that characterizes the orthodox systems. This means that our new systems are integrated.

Accordingly, in imposing our overall condition for general economic consistency on our new systems through our new type of demand and supply functions, we give precedence to the systems' economics over the mathematics of the systems; and this removes the systems' mathematics as a dichotomizing influence from the systems, resulting in the systems being integrated.

On the other hand, orthodox price systems are not subject to our general condition for economic consistency. This results in the economics of the systems becoming subject to the mathematics of the systems. This leads to the systems' mathematics becoming a dichotomizing influence in the orthodox systems. Hence unlike our new systems, the orthodox systems are dichotomized.

8.7 Summary

We discussed how Model A, the orthodox classical system, is initially inconsistent in an economic sense. This is because the behavior in the system, and hence the system's functions, do not ensure that the system is consistent with limitation in resources. Instead, Model A is made consistent with limitation in resources as a result of it being made mathematically consistent.

However, through Model B, we resolved Model A's economic inconsistency as well as how this inconsistency is reflected in Model A in mathematical terms. We also reviewed how we have resolved the hidden inconsistency of Model A, and similar orthodox systems, through generalizing the orthodox approach to microeconomics.

Hence while our new systems have a macroeconomic character, this macroeconomic character stems from our more general approach to microeconomics underlying the systems. Finally, we provided an overview of our new approach to price systems. This brought out how the mathematics of orthodox systems becomes a dichotomizing influence in the latter systems, a problem we avoided in our new systems.

Chapter 9

Resolving The Issue Of Say's Law

9.1 Introduction

We showed in Chapter 6 that Model A, the orthodox form of the classical system, is characterized by an incorrect form of Say's Law. This is a form of the Law that is brought into Model A by the inconsistency we have uncovered in the system; and this incorrect form of the Law restricts Model A to long-run states.

However, in resolving the hidden inconsistency we have uncovered in Model A, through Model B, we brought a correct form of Say's Law into the latter system as was also discussed in Chapter 6. This is a form of the Law that is a true identity hence it cannot possibly restrict Model B to long-run states or restrict the system in any other way.

This will be confirmed in this chapter by our showing more directly that the Law in Model B is indeed a true identity in being simply a descriptive device in the system. Finally, later in the book, in Chapter 17.5, we shall discuss how the rational behavior of Model B accounts for us resolving the issue of Say's Law.

9.2 Remarks On Say's Law

Few concepts in economics have caused such problems as Say's Law, the "Law" that "supply creates its own demand."[17] We are referring to the identity form of the Law that appears in or is implied in various classical writings, and which Keynes and many other economists impute to the classical system.

This form of the Law is represented by an identity between the aggregate demand and aggregate supply of commodities. Becker and Baumol have aptly referred to this identity form of the Law as "Say's Identity." [18] However, we shall

---

[17] On Say's Law see J.B. Say, *A Treatise on Political Economy*, trans. by C.R. Prinsep (1834), pps. 138-39.
[18] G.S. Becker and W.J. Baumol, "The Classical Monetary Theory: The Outcome of the Discussion," *Economica*, XIX (1952), pps. 356-7.

retain the term Say's Law to describe this identity since it is better known in the literature.

Keynes held that Say's Law is the "axiom of parallels" of the classical system; since to Keynes, given the Law, all the other properties of the classical system follow. Hence the Law, to Keynes, was what restricted the classical system to long-run states. [19]

Other economists have also shown that Say's Law gives rise to other problems. This is through the Law preventing money and market processes from being integrated into the system in a consistent manner which invalidly dichotomizes the system into real and monetary parts.[20]

In fact, so problematic has Say's Law become that some economists have attempted to interpret the Law in alternative ways that imply that it is not a part of the classical system or that it is not an identity. This has led to a conflicting literature on the Law.

Patinkin, for example, in his *Money, Interest, And Prices* held that Say's Law is not a basic part of the classical system. Yet Patinkin also recognized that there is evidence that supports the opposite view that the Law is indeed a part of the system.[21] Other conflicting views also characterize parts of the substantial literature on the Law, a literature we cannot cover in any detail here.[22]

We shall find, however, that attempts to interpret Say's Law to show that it is not an identity cannot resolve the issue of the Law. This is because we shall show that the Law is, indeed, an identity or truism. This means that when properly interpreted, it can have no substantive role in a system.

However, the Law, as shown in this book, became a problematic concept in the literature largely because there is an incorrect form of the Law in the orthodox form of the classical system, Model A.

This is due to the hidden inconsistency in the system. This led to a substantive role being imputed to the Law to give the Law an incorrect form in Model A; and this incorrect form of the Law restricts the system to long-run states.

---

[19] Keynes, *op. cit.*, Ch. 2.

[20] See Lange, *op. cit. (1942)*, pps. 49-68 and Patinkin, *op.cit.*, Ch.VIII.

[21] Patinkin, *op. cit.*, p.193. See also Becker and Baumol, *op. cit.*, pps. 371-75 for a discussion that reflects how unclear is the literature on Say's Law.

[22] For summaries of parts of this literature see, for example, Patinkin, *op. cit.*, pps. 645-50 and Becker and Baumol, *op. cit.*, pps. 355-76.

However, this incorrect form of the Law has been removed from our revised classical system, Model B; and as we shall now discuss, it is replaced in the latter system by a correct form of the Law. This is a true identity in being solely a descriptive device in the system.

9.3 Model B's Identity Form Of Say's Law

To show that Model B reflects a true identity form of Say's Law requires drawing on earlier work in the book that appeared in Chapter 6.5. We show Model B again below:

$$\text{Model B}$$

7. $\quad D_j \equiv F_j'[f(z)]$

8. $\quad S_j \equiv G_j'[g(z)]$

9. $\quad E_j'[f(z)-g(z)=0]=0$

There is a budget constraint implicit in the system which is Say's Law. We show the Law again below:

4. $\quad ad \equiv as$

We now enter the aggregate demand (ad) and aggregate supply (as) variables from the Say's Law identity into Model B. This transforms the system into Model B' below:

$$\text{Model B'}$$

7'. $\quad D_j \equiv F_j'[ad, f(z)]$

8'. $\quad S_j \equiv G_j'[as, g(z)]$

9'. $\quad E_j'[(ad \equiv as), f(z) - g(z) = 0] = 0$

Aggregate demand (ad) and aggregate supply (as) reflect the overall volume of commodities that individuals and firms can demand and supply, respectively, as set by the system's budget constraint, which is Say's Law.

Next, functions $f(z)$ and $g(z)$ determine the ratios of the quantities of commodities demanded and the ratios of the quantities of commodities supplied, respectively.

Hence functions $f(z)$ together with aggregate demand (ad) determine the individual quantities of commodities demanded, the D_j. Similarly, functions $g(z)$ together with aggregate supply (as) determine the individual quantities of commodities supplied, the S_j.

We shall now continue to base our analysis on Chapter 6.5 and carry Model B' a further step. Let us, however, first follow Chapter 5.4 and collapse the aggregate demand (ad) and aggregate supply (as) variables in the Say's Law identity into the single variable W.

This variable, to review, reflects the overall flow of output of the system as well as the system's limited resources or budget constraint. Next, we transform both aggregate demand (ad) and aggregate supply (as) in Model B' into the variable W to again form Model B" that was initially introduced in Chapter 6:

Model B"

7". $D_j \equiv F_j'[W, f(z)]$

8". $S_j \equiv G_j'[W, g(z)]$

9". $E_j'[W, f(z) - g(z) = 0] = 0$

We discussed in connection with Model B' how functions $f(z)$ with aggregate demand (ad) determine the individual quantities of commodities demanded, the D_j. Similarly, we discussed how functions $g(z)$ with aggregate supply (as) determine the individual quantities of commodities supplied, the S_j.

Shifting next to Model B" we may now say, in light of how we obtained W, that functions $f(z)$ with W determine the quantities of commodities demanded, the D_j, in the demand functions (7").

Also, again in light of how we obtained W, we may now also say that functions $g(z)$ with W determine the quantities of commodities supplied, the S_j, in the supply functions (8"). We may now readily see that Say's Law in Model B" is a true identity.

When we said that functions $f(z)$ with W determine the quantities demanded, we were taking or describing W as aggregate demand. Similarly, when we said that functions $g(z)$ with W determine the quantities supplied, we were now taking or describing this same W as aggregate supply.

This confirms that the Law in Model B" is a true identity since it simply reflects our describing W alternately as aggregate demand and aggregate supply. Hence since Say's Law is a true identity in Model B", it is also a true identity in Model B since Model B" is only a more detailed form of Model B.

This, of course, explains why the Law is not required to ensure consistency of Model B. This is because in being a true identity, it can have no substantive influence in Model B hence it cannot possibly ensure mathematical consistency of the latter system.

There is, in contrast, an incorrect form of Say's Law in Model A. This is because it is not simply a descriptive device in this latter system as in Model B since it is required to ensure mathematical consistency of Model A. Hence it has a substantive role in the latter system, to explain why there is an incorrect or restricted form of the Law in the system.

9.4 Resolving The Issue Of Say's Law

We resolved the issue of Say's Law through bringing our new approach to the behavior of individuals and firms into our new systems. To review, this new approach to behavior is reflected in us bringing into our new systems, an aspect to behavior that is missing from orthodox systems.

This aspect to behavior is reflected in us taking individuals and firms as being aware that their resources are limited and hence they act in light of this awareness. Next, this aspect to behavior had to be brought into our new type of demand and supply functions. This was done in the following way.

This aspect to behavior has two facets: First, that individuals and firms are aware that their resources are limited; and second, they act in light of this awareness. Moreover, both of these facets to our new approach to behavior are brought simultaneously into Model B" by the interior functions $f(z)$ and $g(z)$; and this explains why our new approach to the behavior of individuals and firms resolved the issue of Say's Law.

Functions $f(z)$ and $g(z)$, given that individuals and firms are aware that their resources are limited, reflect how they act in light of this awareness. There was next the issue as to how individuals and firms are made aware that their resources are limited; and as would be expected, functions $f(z)$ and $g(z)$ also ensured this.

This was through these functions ridding Model B" of Model A's incorrect form of Say's Law. This incorrect form of the Law had led to the variable W being put outside the behavioral content of Model A.

However, W is brought into the behavioral content of Model B" where it reflects how individuals and firms are made aware that their resources are limited; and it was in bringing W into the behavioral content of Model B" that we brought a correct form of Say's Law into the system.

This is because W, in being brought into the behavioral content of Model B", rid the Law of the invalid elements and role described in Chapter 6.7, that characterize the Law in Model A and which bring an incorrect form of the Law into the latter system.

Hence the Law in Model B", in being rid of these invalid elements and role, was transformed into a correct form in the latter system. We may illustrate how this was accomplished in the following way. Let us drop functions $f(z)$ and $g(z)$ from Model B" hence dropping our new approach to behavior from the system.

This means that we must now replace the demand and supply functions of Model B" with those of Model A to hence transform Model B" into Model A. Let us now focus on what happens to the variable W in Model B" although we first need to refer to Model A..

Model A is initially inconsistent in a mathematical sense; and mathematical consistency is then ensured by Say's Law being imposed on the system to eliminate a surplus equation. This means that to see exactly what happens to the W in Model B", we must reverse the whole process whereby we brought a correct form of the Law into Model B".

That is, we must take the variable W from the demand and supply functions of Model B" and reverse how W was formed by collapsing the aggregate demand and supply variables in the Say's Law identity into the single variable W. Hence we return to the initial Say's Law identity, namely, $ad \equiv as$.

This identity, following orthodox analysis, is then imposed on Model A to make the system mathematically consistent. This means, however, that the Law is misused in Model A since in being an identity, it should not be given a substantive role in a system. However, it is given the substantive role of making Model A mathematically consistent to hence bring an incorrect form of the Law into the system.

This is a form of the Law that is given an external character in being made to act as a budget constraint that is imposed from the outside on Model A to make the system mathematically consistent; and this removes W from within the behavioral content of Model B" to put it outside the behavioral content of Model A.

Consequently, in resolving the issue of Say's Law through functions $f(z)$ and $g(z)$, we rid the Say's Law of Model B" of the incorrect external character given to the Law in Model A on account of the Law being required to make the latter system mathematically consistent.

This resulted in the variable W, which was formed from the correct Say's Law of Model B", entering the behavioral content of the latter system in entering the system's demand and supply functions.

This was the means whereby individuals and firms are made aware in Model B" that their resources are limited; and this required that the Say's Law in Model B" be rid of the invalid elements and role that characterize Model A's incorrect form of the Law. This explains why a correct form of the Law characterizes Model B".

9.5 Summary

Model A, the orthodox form of the classical system, is characterized by an incorrect form of Say's Law. This is brought into the system by the inconsistency we have uncovered in the system; and this incorrect form of the Law restricts Model A to long-run states.

However, in resolving Model A's inconsistency through Model B, we brought a correct form of the Law into the latter system. This is a form of the Law which, as we confirmed in this chapter, is a true identity. Hence it cannot possibly restrict Model B to long-run states.

This was accomplished by our bringing our new approach to the behavior of individuals and firms into our new systems, as represented by Model B, to rid Model A of inconsistency. Finally, later in the book, in Chapter 17.5, we shall discuss how the rational behavior of Model B accounts for us resolving the issue of Say's Law.

Chapter 10

The Macroeconomic Character Of The New Systems

10.1 Introduction

This chapter will bring out more fully the nature of our new systems' macroeconomic character as well as the nature of the systems' budget constraints.

We discussed earlier how the systems are characterized by a behaviorally-determined overall output or income variable that accounts for the systems having a macroeconomic character. Moreover, this overall output variable also reflects the systems' limited resources or budget constraints.

Next, the systems' market processes determine the systems' overall output. Hence these market processes also necessarily determine the systems' budget constraints. This means that these budget constraints, in being by determined by the systems' market processes, are determined internally in the systems.

As a result, these budget constraints cannot restrict the systems to any particular states. Hence the systems will move to alternative states as behavior changes, reflecting how the systems have a macroeconomic character. Yet the systems are microeconomic systems in being based wholly on the behavior of the individual and the firm.

Whereas orthodox systems such as Model A are subject to externally-imposed budget constraints. These, however, restrict the systems to specific states, the systems' macroeconomic character hence being suppressed.

10.2 There Is A Microeconomic Basis To Model B's Macroeconomic Character

Model B, our revised classical system, reflects a more general approach to microeconomics compared to Model A, the orthodox classical system; and we arrived at this more general approach to microeconomics of Model B through resolving the hidden inconsistency we uncovered in Model A.

This was through our bringing into Model B, an aspect to the behavior of individuals and firms that is missing from Model A. Moreover, Model B's microeconomics led to the system having a macroeconomic character.

Model B, as we showed earlier, is rid of an incorrect form of Say's Law that restricts Model A to long-run states. Hence Model B is not restricted in this way, which means that the system will move to alternative states as behavior changes. This gives Model B a macroeconomic character but only in principle; and this brings up another key facet to macroeconomic systems.

This is reflected in macroeconomic systems having a behaviorally-determined overall output or income variable. Hence as behavior changes, this will change overall output or income to actually cause the system to move to alternative states.

However, the Keynesian system's overall output or income variable W is macroeconomic in character. This is reflected in it being determined by aggregate demand and supply functions; but these functions suppress the microeconomics of the real part of the Keynesian system.

Model B also has to have a behaviorally-determined overall output or income variable. However, this variable in Model B must be consistent with microeconomics since Model B is microeconomic in character; and Model B's overall output variable W is consistent with the system's microeconomics.

This is because Model B's W does not directly enter the market processes of the system as is the case with the W of the Keynesian system. Instead, Model B's overall output variable W enters the system as a budget or income constraint.

Next, Model B's interior functions operate on W to determine individual quantities of commodities demanded and supplied reflecting how the system is microeconomic in character. Yet Model B, as we have discussed, also has a macroeconomic.

This analysis brings out how there is a parallel between the Keynesian system and Model B with regard to how the systems are given a macroeconomic character. Yet Model B is more general than the Keynesian system.

As we discussed in Chapter 5.3, to form a macroeconomic system, we must form a system that, in the first place, is consistent, in principle, with being able to move among alternative states as behavior changes.

This is accomplished through the system being rid of Model A's incorrect form of Say's Law that restricts this system to long-run states. Moreover, the system must also be characterized by a behaviorally-determined overall output or income variable;

and both the Keynesian system and Model B reflect these properties.

That is, both of these systems are rid of Model A's form of Says Law and, as well both systems are characterized by behaviorally determined overall output or income variables. Moreover, these properties are consistent with each other in both Model B and the Keynesian system, in that both systems meet our condition for such consistency set out in Chapter 5.3.

This reflects how both systems are internally consistent macroeconomic systems. Yet the Keynesian system has a restricted character compared to Model B

This is because the properties we have described are brought into the Keynesian system through macroeconomic analysis; and this suppresses the microeconomics of the real part of the Keynesian system. Whereas these properties are brought into Model B through microeconomic analysis; and this accounts for Model B being a wholly microeconomic system.

10.3 Budget Constraints In Price Systems

Price systems based on our new approach to the systems are wholly rid of any restrictions on their behavior or economic rationale stemming from the mathematics of the systems. This is reflected, as illustrated by Model B, in our not having to impose mathematical consistency on this system; since this would restrict the system's behavior or economic rationale as is the case with Model A.

Instead, Model B's demand and supply functions, and hence the system's behavior or economic rationale, automatically ensures that the system is consistent in a mathematical sense as we discussed in Chapter 6.4.

This means that mathematical consistency of Model B is a consequence of economic consistency which confirms that the system's mathematics cannot possibly restrict the system's behavior in any way. Let us contrast this with Model A.

This latter system's functions do not ensure that the system is consistent with limitation in resources; and this results in the system being initially inconsistent in a mathematical sense. Next, Say's Law is imposed on Model A to make the system mathematically consistent; and the Law is thereby transformed into a budget constraint that ensures that the system is consistent with limitation in resources.

However, we discussed in the previous chapter how we have rid Model B of Model A's budget constraint form of Say's

Law. This was then replaced in Model B with a true identity form of the Law. This is a form of the Law that can have no substantive influence on Model B hence it cannot possibly be the system's budget constraint.

Nonetheless, Model B has to be subject to a budget constraint; and we shall now discuss the nature of the system's budget constraint, which we shall refer to as the system's true budget constraint. This is a type of budget constraint that is determined internally in Model B by the system's market processes.

10.4 The True Or Internal Budget Constraints Of Model B

Let us proceed by assuming that we use the method on which Model B is based to form a short-run system. However, we bear in mind that we focus in this book on the general economic logic of price systems.

Hence while we refer to short-run systems in this and other chapters of the book, we are referring only to the general economic logic of the systems and hence to properties that stem from this general economic logic; and this general logic is derived from Model B.

Consequently, short-run systems that are based on the similar approach as Model B will, in reflecting a similar general economic logic as Model B, also be characterized, like Model B, by budget constraints that reflect the overall output or income of the systems.

Now we have discussed earlier in the book how it is the rational behavior of individuals and firms that results in the overall output or income of Model B, that we denote by W, being taken by individuals and firms to reflect their limited resources or budget constraint. However, a further stage to this analysis is required.

This is to show that Model B's overall output, and hence the system's resources or budget constraint, are limited in short-run states by the operation of the system's market equilibrating processes. This will cast light on the system's budget constraint and the system's macroeconomic character.

Let us consider the short-run system referred to earlier that is based on the same approach that characterizes Model B. We also assume that the price mechanism operates in this short-run system in a manner that sets overall output below the full-employment level.

Hence the behavior of the price system sets a limit or constraint on overall output or income. This is because a more efficient working of the price system would set overall output at a higher level.

This imposing of a limit on overall output or income is generally analogous to imposing a budget constraint on the system, albeit a short-run budget constraint, that sets overall output or income below a full-employment level.

This is because the price mechanism prevents the resources of the system from being more fully employed. However, this limit or budget constraint is not imposed on the system from the outside. Instead, it is determined endogenously in our new system on account of the working of the system's price mechanism.

Hence our new systems, as it were, subject themselves to budget constraints in short-run states. This is through their behavior, as reflected in operation of the systems' market processes determining, at any date, the overall output or income of the systems.

This overall output or income constitutes the systems' true or internally-determined budget constraints. This overall output or income, on account of the rational behavior of individuals and firms, then enters the demand and supply functions of the systems as a budget constraint as will be confirmed through Model B in Section 10.6 below.

10.5 Further Remarks On The Internal Budget Constraints Of Model B

Let us again refer to our short-run system that we form using the same approach as Model B. Next, we also assume that this short-run system moves through a series of short-run equilibria towards a long-run, full-employment state.

This means that in each short-run equilibrium the system, as it were, creates its own budget constraint in determining some level of overall output. These are short-run budget constraints since we are assuming that in short-run equilibrium, overall output is below the full-employment level.

Hence these short-run budget constraints arise as a result of the inefficiency of the price mechanism in determining overall output. Let us next assume that the system reaches a long-run, full-employment state.

This means that it now becomes subject to a long-run budget constraint which the system itself has also created in now setting overall output at a full-employment level; and we may also attribute this long-run budget constraint to the operation of the price mechanism. However, this now reflects the efficiency rather than the inefficiency with which the price mechanism operates in now setting overall output at a full-employment level.

Hence the budget constraints of our new systems, whether the systems are in long or short-run states, become variables that are determined endogenously in the systems by the behavior of the systems as reflected in the operation of the systems' market processes.

Specifically, by the efficiency or inefficiency with which the systems' market processes operate in determining the overall output or income of the systems, this overall output or income constituting the systems' true budget constraints.

Clearly, however, in more detailed forms of Model B, we would need to spell out more precisely, how the behavior of the systems' market processes influences the level of overall output or income of the systems. In particular, we would need to spell out in detail the nature of the short-run market processes implied in our analysis. These analyses, however, are beyond the scope of the present book.

10.6 Model B's Internal Budget Constraints And The System's Macroeconomic Character

Model B's overall output is determined by the system's market processes; and this overall output or income also reflects the system's budget constraint. Hence the system's budget constraint, like the system's overall output, is determined internally in the system by these market processes. Let us review this analysis through Model B" which is shown below:

Model B"

7". $D_j \equiv F_j'[W, f(z)]$

8". $S_j \equiv G_j'[W, g(z)]$

9". $E_j'[W, f(z) - g(z) = 0] = 0$

We denoted the overall output of Model B" by the variable W; and this variable enters the system as a budget constraint. This is reflected in W being within the system's demand and supply functions, functions (7") and (8"). Then the interior functions $f(z)$ and $g(z)$ that are within these demand and supply functions operate on W to determine the individual quantities of commodities demanded and supplied.

This reflects how Model B" is a microeconomic system, the system hence being characterized by microeconomic market processes. Yet the system is characterized by the aggregative or macroeconomic variable W. Let us review how this variable arises in the system.

We have discussed in Chapter 6.9 how the demand and supply functions of Model B" imply that individuals and firms determine their demands and supplies in the knowledge or awareness that their resources are limited.

As a result, individuals and firms need to know their overall volume of resources in order to determine the quantities of commodities they demand and supply. Let us now assume that the system reaches equilibrium with a set of individual quantities being determined.

These quantities constitute the resources of individuals and firms, these resources hence being in terms of individual quantities of commodities. Next, since individuals and firms need to know their overall resources, there is utility to them of a variable that reflects their overall resources or budget constraint.

Hence individuals and firms themselves create the variable W that reflects their overall resources or budget constraint. This variable is a summation of the individual quantities of commodities that constitute the resources of individuals and firms.

Consequently, Model B's budget constraint W is created by individuals and firms themselves; and this budget constraint then enters the system's demand and supply functions.

Then the interior functions $f(z)$ and $g(z)$ within the system's demand and supply functions operate on W to determine the individual quantities of commodities demanded and supplied, reflecting how the system is microeconomic in character.

Next, assuming that the system reaches a further equilibrium, a new budget constraint variable W is again created in the manner described; and this also enters Model B's demand and supply functions as a budget constraint.

As a result, a behaviorally-determined macroeconomic variable W, that reflects both the overall output and budget constraint of the system, is created in every equilibrium described by Model B". This gives the system a macroeconomic character even though the system is a microeconomic system in being based wholly on the behavior of the individual and the firm.

10.7 Budget Identities And Budget Constraints In Price Systems

In resolving the hidden inconsistency of Model A, we arrived at an approach to price systems that bases the systems solely on the behavior in the systems. This is because behavior in the new systems, as illustrated by Model B, is not restricted by the systems' mathematics. This is because mathematical consistency of the systems is a consequence of economic consistency.

Hence behavior in the systems freely operates with no restriction whatsoever from mathematical elements. Whereas Model A's mathematics restricts the system's behavior or economic rationale. This assists us in understanding Say's Law.

Through resolving the hidden inconsistency of Model A, we formed Model B that is characterized, as we showed in Chapter 9, by a true identity form of the Law. Next, behavior in the system is long-run behavior that moves the system to a long-run, full-employment state.

This raised the question of what is Model B's budget constraint. This is because we had rid this system of the external budget-constraint form of Say's Law that is imposed on Model A to make this system consistent.

Clearly, Model B's budget constraint could not be Say's Law since the Law is an identity or truism in the system hence it can have no substantive influence in the system. Yet the Law provided a clue as to what is Model B's true budget constraint.

As discussed, Say's Law cannot be Model B's budget constraint. However, it describes the system's true budget constraint which is the overall output of the system; and this overall output is set at a full-employment level in the system.

Next, it is behavior in the system, as reflected in operation of the system's market processes, that ensures that resources are fully-employed.

This means that Say's Law in Model B is a description of the consequences of the free and efficient operation of the system's market processes as reflected in these processes determining the overall long-run output of the system.

Hence we see how Say's Law, although being an identity or truism, led us to find what is Model B's true budget constraint; since we found that the Law is a description of the system's true budget constraint, namely, the overall output or income of the system.

Moreover, we may go beyond the long-run Model B where the Law applies, to short-run systems based on the same approach as Model B; since these latter systems are also characterized by identities that are similar to Model B's Say's Law.

This is because the same analysis that applied to the long-run Model B, and Say's Law, also applies to short-run or macroeconomic systems based on a similar approach as Model B. Hence as in Model B, behavior in our new short-run systems is not restricted by the systems' mathematics.

Consequently, our new short-run systems will describe various short-run states where overall output is below the full-employment level.

This reflects how these systems, unrestricted by mathematical elements, fully accommodate short-run behavior just as Model B, also unrestricted by mathematical elements, fully accommodates that system's long-run behavior.

These short-run systems will also, like Model B, be characterized by budget identities, the counterparts to the true Say's Law of Model B; and these identities will also describe the overall output or income in various short-run states the systems may describe, this overall output or income reflecting the true budget constraints of the systems.

Next, overall output is a result of the behavior in the systems as reflected in the operation of the price mechanism.

This means that the systems' budget identities, in describing these various levels of overall output or income, will always automatically adapt to reflect or describe the consequences of behavior of the price mechanism, as reflected in this behavior determining various levels of overall output.

As a result, the systems' budget identities simply describe the systems' true budget constraints, namely, the overall output or income that emerges in various states that the systems may describe. Hence we find that Say's Law is a special case of budget identities that characterize all price systems based on our new approach to the systems.

10.8 Summary

This chapter discussed how our new price systems, which we represent by Model B, are characterized by internally-determined budget constraints. These are constraints that reflect the overall output or income of the systems. This was best seen by referring to short-run states but our analysis also applied when our new systems reach long-run equilibrium.

To review, we assumed that the operation of the systems' market processes sets overall output in short-run states below the full employment level; and we took this as generally equivalent to imposing a short-run budget constraint on the systems. This is because a more efficient operation of the price mechanism would set overall output at a higher level.

Moreover, since overall output is determined in our new systems by the operation of the systems' market processes, and overall output of the new systems reflects the systems' budget constraints, the systems' budget constraints are determined internally in the systems. Hence they cannot restrict the systems to any particular states.

Whereas orthodox systems such as Model A are characterized by externally-imposed budget constraints; but these restrict the systems to particular states, a reflection of the systems' macroeconomic character being suppressed.

However, through our new systems' internal budget constraints, we internalize in these new systems, the external budget constraints that are imposed on orthodox systems but which restrict the latter systems to specific states.

Consequently, our new systems can move freely among alternative states as behavior changes, unrestricted by externally-imposed budget constraints such as characterize orthodox systems. This reflects how the new systems have a macroeconomic character.

Moreover, these internal budget constraints are consistent with the systems being wholly microeconomic in character; since these budget constraints provide the basis for the maximizing behavior of the individual and the firm. Hence our new systems, while having a macroeconomic character, are microeconomic systems. This is because they are based wholly on the behavior of the individual and the firm.

Chapter 11

Generalizing Microeconomic And Macroeconomic Price Systems

11.1 Introduction

Through resolving the hidden inconsistency of Model A, through Model B we have, as was discussed in Chapter 8.5, generalized the orthodox approach to microeconomic analysis that is the basis of Model A. Hence Model B reflects a more general approach to microeconomics compared to Model A.

Moreover, this resulted in Model B being able to move into short-run states as behavior changes, to give the system a macroeconomic character. This is because Model B is rid of an incorrect form of Say's Law that characterizes Model A and which restricts the latter system to long-run states.

Consequently, the short-run systems that emerge from Model B as behavior in the latter system changes will, like Model B, also reflect our more general form of microeconomics. As a result, we extend, in principle, this more general approach to microeconomics to short-run or macroeconomic systems.

We shall also discuss how macroeconomic or aggregative variables of the Keynesian system and Model B differ; and as well, we shall contrast Keynes' and the new approach to the issue of the restriction of the classical system to long-run states.

11.2 Resolving Model A's Hidden Inconsistency

Model A, the orthodox classical system, is initially inconsistent in a mathematical sense. Moreover, we showed that this is due to the system being inconsistent in an economic sense. This is because the system's functions do not ensure that the system is consistent with limitation in resources.

This, in turn, results in the system being initially inconsistent in a mathematical sense. Next, Say's Law is imposed on the system to make it mathematically consistent; and this ensures that the system is consistent with limitation in resources. This could be seen in the following way.

We collapsed the aggregate demand and supply variables in the Say's Law identity of Model A into the single variable W. This variable reflects the overall output of the system; and as we discussed in Chapter 5, it also represents the system's limited resources or budget constraint.

Hence W is imposed on Model A from the outside through Say's Law; and since W also reflects the limited resources of the system, the system is thereby made consistent with limitation in resources. Nonetheless, the system is inconsistent in an economic sense.

This is because consistency with limited resources should instead be ensured by the behavior of the individual and the firm and hence by the system's demand and supply functions; and this is the case with Model B's functions since these ensure that the latter system is consistent with limitation in resources.

As a result, we resolved, through Model B, Model A's economic inconsistency. Moreover, we thereby also resolved through Model B, how this inconsistency is reflected in Model A in mathematical terms.

This is because mathematical consistency of Model B is a consequence of economic consistency. Whereas mathematical consistency is given precedence over economic consistency in Model A in ensuring that the system is consistent with limitation in resources.

11.3 Suppression Of The Microeconomics Of The Real Part Of The Keynesian System

Keynes' macroeconomic system is restricted in generality because, unlike our new systems, it does not have a satisfactory basis in microeconomics. To review, we arrived at our more general approach to microeconomics that characterizes Model B by resolving the inconsistency we uncovered in the microeconomics of Model A.

Moreover, through this new approach to microeconomics, we also simultaneously rid Model B of an incorrect form of Say's Law that restricts Model A to long-run states. Hence Model B is not restricted to long-run states but will move to short-run states were behavior to change to short-run behavior, the system hence having a macroeconomic character.

This means that the short-run forms that Model B may take as behavior in the system changes will also be characterized, like Model B, by our more general microeconomics. Hence we extend this more general microeconomics to short-run or macroeconomic systems. Let us go further into this analysis.

Model B, in having a macroeconomic character, is characterized by a behaviorally-determined overall output or income variable; and this is also the case with the Keynesian system.

Next, as we have shown, the overall output or income of Model B reflects an internally-determined budget constraint in the system; and this internally-determined budget constraint of Model B is relevant to or consistent with microeconomics.

This is because Model B's overall output or income variable, W, is brought as a budget constraint into the system's demand and supply functions by the interior functions $f(z)$ and $g(z)$. These functions then operate on this W to determine the individual quantities of commodities demanded and supplied. Clearly, this gives Model B a microeconomic character.

However, this process whereby Model B is given a microeconomic character is missing from the Keynesian system. This is because the Keynesian system's overall output W does not enter the behavioral content of the system as a budget constraint of relevance to microeconomics as in Model B.

Instead, W directly enters the market processes of the Keynesian system to be determined by aggregate demand and supply functions. However, these functions suppress or abstract from the microeconomics of the real part of the Keynesian system.

11.4 Macroeconomic Or Aggregative Variables In Price Systems

We have discussed how the overall output or income variable W in the Keynesian system directly enters the system's market processes, to be determined by aggregate demand and supply functions; and aggregative variables such as W assist us in viewing the price system in overall or macroeconomic terms.

Hence there is utility in this sense in forming a macroeconomic or aggregative variable such as the Keynesian W.

However, such aggregative variables in macroeconomic systems such as the Keynesian system have no basis for their existence in the behavior of the individual and the firm. On the other hand, the aggregative variable W in Model B has a rationale for its existence in the behavior of the individual and the firm.

As we discussed in Chapter 6.9, there is a more general approach to rational behavior in Model B compared to the orthodox approach. This rational behavior in Model B is reflected in individuals and firms determining the quantities of commodities they demand and supply in the knowledge or awareness that their resources are limited.

Hence there is utility to individuals and firms of a variable that reflects their overall resources.

This gives rise to the aggregative variable W that reflects their overall resources; since W is a summation of the flow of the individual quantities of commodities that we take as constituting the limited resources or budget constraint of individuals and firms.

Consequently, the rationale for the existence of the macroeconomic or aggregative variable W in Model B stems from the rational behavior of the individual and the firm.

Whereas the rationale for the existence of the overall output variable W in the Keynesian system does not stem from the rational behavior of the individual and the firm. This difference between the systems is also reflected in the following way.

We have discussed how the Keynesian W directly enters the market processes of the Keynesian system. However, this Keynesian W suppresses the microeconomics of the real part of the system, hence it is inconsistent with microeconomics. This is a reflection of how the rationale of the Keynesian W does not stem from the behavior of the individual and the firm.

In contrast, the overall output variable W of Model B enters the system's demand and supply functions as a budget constraint that is of relevance to microeconomics. Hence it is consistent with the system's microeconomic character. This is a reflection of how the W of Model B stems from the behavior of the individual and the firm.

11.5 The Unifying Influence Of Consistency With Limitation In Resources In The New Systems

As discussed earlier in the book, in making Model A mathematically consistent, we are able to solve for the equilibrium quantities and prices of the system. Moreover, the quantities we solve for must sum to the limited volume of resources of the system.

This means that in making Model A mathematically consistent, we make the system consistent with limitation in resources. However, Model A is simultaneously made subject to limitation in resources as a consequence of being made mathematically consistent.

This is because Say's Law which is imposed on Model A to make the system mathematically consistent, also acts as a long-run budget constraint. This restricts Model A to long-run states to hence suppress the macroeconomic character of the system.

However, we separated out in Model B how the system is made consistent with limitation in resources and how it is made subject to limitation in resources.

Then Model B is made consistent with limitation in resources by one aspect to the behavior of the system with the system being made subject to limitation in resources by another aspect to the behavior of Model B.

To review, we first transformed Model A's demand and supply functions into the functions of Model B; and these latter functions ensure that behavior in Model B is consistent with limitation in resources. Hence consistency with limitation in resources is correctly ensured in Model B in being ensured by the behavior of the individual and the firm.

Moreover, Model B, of course, is also necessarily subject to limitation in resources. However, Model B's functions rid the system of Model A's long-run budget constraint form of Say's Law. Hence Model B is not made subject to limitation in resources by the Law. This means that Model B is not restricted to long-run states as is the case with Model A.

This allowed us to also correctly ensure how Model B is made subject to limitation in resources.

This, as was discussed in Chapter 10, is through Model B being made subject to limitation in resources by an internally-determined budget constraint; and this budget constraint cannot restrict the system to long-run states.

This is because this internal budget constraint reflects the overall output or income of the system. Hence since the system's overall output or income is determined by the operation of the system's market equilibrating processes, the system's budget constraint is also determined by the system's market processes.

Consequently, Model B's budget constraint cannot restrict the system to long-run states. As a result, the system will move into short-run states as behavior changes to short-run behavior. This gives Model B a macroeconomic character whereas the macroeconomic character of Model A is suppressed.

Hence short-run or macroeconomic systems emerge from Model B; and these latter systems, like Model B, will necessarily reflect the more general approach to microeconomics that characterizes Model B. This brings a unity to microeconomic and macroeconomic systems in terms of the systems' general economic logic; and this accounts for Model B providing the basis to integrate these systems.

11.6 Alternative Approaches To The Classical System

Keynes showed that the orthodox classical system, which we represent by Model A, is restricted by Say's Law to long-run states. This, as we have shown, is because the Law is imposed on the system to make it mathematically consistent; and the Law imposes the overall output or income variable W on the system. This is a long-run overall output or income which hence restricts Model A to long-run states.

However, the solution to this restriction of Model A to long-run states is quite different between the Keynesian system and Model B. Keynes focused on giving the overall output or income variable W of his system a behavioral character, by removing Model A's Say's Law from his system.

This gives his system a macroeconomic character; but this is through macroeconomic analysis which results in the microeconomics of the real part of the Keynesian system being suppressed.

In contrast, we came upon a more general approach to microeconomics through resolving the hidden inconsistency of Model A; and we based Model B on this more general approach to microeconomics. This meant that we also removed Model A's Say's Law from Model B but through microeconomic analysis.

This, as was discussed in Chapter 5.3, gave Model B a macroeconomic character but only in principle. This is because Model B also had to be characterized by a behaviorally-determined overall output or income variable. This is required so that Model B may also have an actual means whereby it is made to move among alternative states.

Moreover, this behaviorally-determined W of Model B also had to be consistent with the microeconomic character of the system. This was ensured by the W of Model B also taking on the meaning of reflecting the system's limited resources or budget constraint; since this ensured that this W is consistent with Model B's microeconomic character.

Hence both Model B and the Keynesian system have a macroeconomic character. However, the microeconomics of the real part of the Keynesian system is suppressed. Whereas Model B is a wholly microeconomic system.

11.7 Further Remarks On Why The Inconsistency Of Model A Remained Hidden

Clearly, our giving a behavioral meaning to the overall output variable W of Model A, through Model B, was a key element in our resolving the inconsistency of Model A. However, the overall output variable W does not appear explicitly in Model A; and this contributed to this inconsistency remaining hidden.

Hence to resolve this inconsistency, we first had to make overall output of Model A explicit. This, as we saw in Chapter 5.4, was done through our collapsing the aggregate demand and supply variables in the Say's Law identity to form the single variable W that reflects the system's overall output or income.

Next, having elicited W in Model A, we found that it was brought incorrectly into the system. This is because it is imposed on the system from the outside by Say's Law in order to make the system mathematically consistent.

This means that since the long-run volume of overall output, W, is imposed on Model A from the outside, this W is non-behavioral in character. This, in the first place, restricts Model A to long-run states. Moreover, we were also able to see that the system is inconsistent and to provide a solution to this inconsistency.

We have discussed earlier how the variable W in Model A, while reflecting the system's overall output or income, also reflects the system's limited resources or budget constraint. This, in turn, allowed us to see that there is an inconsistency in the system; since it became evident that consistency with limitation in resources was ensured incorrectly in Model A.

This is because it is ensured by the system being made mathematically consistent rather than by the behavior of the individual and the firm. This, of course, is the inconsistency we uncovered in Model A.

We then resolved this inconsistency through Model B; since consistency of the latter system with limited resources is ensured by the behavior of the individual and the firm. This was through our bringing the aspect to the behavior of the individual and the firm we have described earlier, into Model B, an aspect to behavior that is missing from Model A.

This resulted in Model B having a more general microeconomic character compared to Model A. Moreover, this also led to Model B having a macroeconomic character in that Model B can move to alternative states as behavior changes.

Hence the system's macroeconomic character, reflected in it being able to move to alternative states, emerges out of the more general microeconomics that characterizes the system. This explained why through Model B, we rid the latter system of the microeconomic-macroeconomic dichotomy that characterizes Model A.

11.8 Summary

We first reviewed in this chapter how we resolved the hidden inconsistency of Model A through Model B; and we thereby generalized the orthodox microeconomic analysis underlying Model A to hence base Model B on a more general approach to microeconomics compared to Model A.

Moreover, in resolving the hidden inconsistency of Model A, we also rid Model B of an incorrect form of Say's Law that restricts Model A to long-run states. Hence Model B is not restricted to long-run states but will move into short-run states were behavior to change to short-run behavior.

This means that the short-run systems that emerge from Model B when behavior in the latter system changes, will also reflect the more general approach to microeconomics that characterizes Model B. Whereas the Keynesian short-run system is dichotomized from the orthodox classical long-run system. Moreover, the microeconomics of the real part of the Keynesian system is suppressed.

We also discussed how the macroeconomic or aggregative variables of the Keynesian system and Model B differ; and as well, we contrasted Keynes' and the new approach to the issue of the restriction of the classical system to long-run states.

Chapter 12

Market Processes In The Revised Price Systems

12.1 Introduction

We have in this book taken Model A to represent the orthodox classical system; and we focused on Keynes' criticism that the system is restricted to long-run states. Next, we resolved this problem through Model B.

This is a system which, as we discussed in Chapter 10, is characterized by market equilibrating processes. These are microeconomic market processes, since Model B is microeconomic in character. However, we have also discussed how Patinkin has shown that Model A, which he took as a neoclassical system, is subject to an invalid real-monetary dichotomy and an indeterminate price level.

As a result, it is implied that these problems with Model A have been resolved through Model B; and this is the case as will be established in this chapter through a monetary form of Model B, to be referred to as Model C.

12.2 A Monetary Form Of The Revised Classical System

Model B, our revised classical system, is shown below:

Model B

7. $\quad D_j \equiv F_j'[f(z)]$

8. $\quad S_j \equiv G_j'[g(z)]$

9. $\quad E_j'[f(z)-g(z)=0]=0$

Model B's demand and supply functions are real long-run relative demand and supply functions. These functions contrast with monetary long-run relative demand and supply functions which will now be developed as a basis for Model C.

These latter functions, like Model B's functions, are also based on interior functions. However, these are not now real interior functions such as characterize Model B. Instead, they are monetary interior functions which are shown below:

$$10. \qquad R_1 \equiv f_1(K)$$

$$11. \qquad S_1 \equiv g_1(P)$$

The variable R_1 is the ratio of the quantity of money demanded for transactions purposes to the overall demand for commodities, the latter being measured in money.

This ratio, as is shown in (10), is made a function of the Cambridge K that characterizes the well-known Cambridge cash-balance approach to the long-run quantity theory of money. Next, the variable S_1 is the ratio of the fixed money supply to the overall supply of commodities, the latter also being measured in money.

This latter ratio depends on the price level, P, as shown in (11); since the overall supply of commodities, when measured in money, will vary with P which will change the ratio S_1.

Clearly, the monetary interior functions are derived from a long-run quantity theory of money equation, specifically, from the Cambridge cash-balance approach to this theory. Let us now substitute the monetary interior functions, functions $f_1(K)$ and $g_1(P)$, into functions (7) and (8) of Model B.

This leads to the demand and supply functions, functions (12) and (13), of our new long-run monetary system, Model C, that is shown below. Moreover, the system is characterized by excess-demand equations, equations (14) which are derived from the system's demand and supply functions:

Model C

$$12. \qquad D_j \equiv F_j''[f_1(K), f(z)]$$

$$13. \qquad S_j \equiv G_j''[g_1(P), g(z)]$$

$$14. \qquad E_j''[f_1(K) - g_1(P) = 0, f(z) - g(z) = 0] = 0$$

As is the case with Model B, we have also imposed on Model C a condition for general economic consistency on the system, namely, that consistency with limited resources be ensured by the system's behavior or economic rationale.

This is through our bringing the aspect to the behavior of individuals and firms discussed earlier in the book, that is missing from orthodox systems, into Model C. This results in the quantities of goods that are determined in Model C by the system's functions being relative quantities as in Model B.

Hence as in Model B, the quantities in Model C, in being relative quantities, will adjust in a relative manner so as to always sum to the total of the system's limited resources, resources which in Model C now include money.

This ensures that behavior in Model C, as is also the case with Model B, is necessarily behavior that is consistent with limitation in resources.

12.3 Consistency Of The New Long-Run Monetary System

Model C, the monetary form of Model B, is shown again below:

Model C

12. $\quad D_j \equiv F_j''[f_1(K), f(z)]$

13. $\quad S_j \equiv G_j''[g_1(P), g(z)]$

14. $\quad E_j''[f_1(K) - g_1(P) = 0, f(z) - g(z) = 0] = 0$

Model C must be interpreted in the same way in which we interpreted Model B. That is, the overall excess-demand equations $E_j''[]=0$ in (14) determine the market behavior of the system in determining the excess-demands that enter the system's markets.

However, the overall excess-demand equations $E_j''[]=0$ themselves, and hence the market behavior of the system, is a function of or is constrained by the elements that are internal to these overall functions.

These internal elements, in turn, stem from our new approach to the behavior of individuals and firms; and this behavior ensures that Model C is automatically consistent in a mathematical sense.

Let us assume that the overall conditions $E_j''[]=0$ in (14) vanish, the system hence being in general equilibrium. This is only possible were both internal conditions within conditions $E_j''[]=0$ to vanish.

We also next assume that the monetary condition, namely, condition $f_1(K) - g_1(P) = 0$, first vanishes, allowing us to solve for the price level, P.

There are now the real conditions, namely, conditions $f(z) - g(z) = 0$, remaining within (14); and the vanishing of these conditions, which are $(n-1)$ in number, determines the $(n-1)$ relative prices, the z.

Moreover, the vanishing of these latter conditions causes the overall conditions in (14) to now vanish, the system hence being in general equilibrium. Consequently, P and the z are determined in general equilibrium. As well, they are determined independently of each other, reflecting how money is neutral in the system.

As a result, Model C is automatically consistent in a mathematical sense; and this is a result of the system being based on our new approach to price systems.

We may also look on Model C as being characterized by the following monetary equilibrium condition: this is a condition that is reflected in equality between the ratio of the quantity of money demanded to the overall quantity of commodities demanded and the ratio of the quantity of money supplied to the overall quantity of commodities supplied.

Then we substitute the monetary interior functions, functions (10) and 11), into this equilibrium condition to form the monetary condition $f_1(K)-g_1(P)=0$ from which we solve for the price level.

There is then a set of $(n-1)$ real equilibrium conditions reflecting equality between the ratios of the quantities of commodities demanded across the system with the ratios of the quantities of commodities supplied.

We then substitute the real interior functions, functions $f(z)$ and $g(z)$, into these equilibrium conditions to form conditions $f(z)-g(z)=0$. These latter conditions, to review, are $(n-1)$ in number hence they allow us to solve for the $(n-1)$ relative prices.

12.4 Resolving The Price Level Indeterminacy Of The Neoclassical System

Model C's excess-demand equations are shown again below:

14. $\qquad E_j''[f_1(K)-g_1(P)=0, f(z)-g(z)=0]=0$

Let us hold the relative commodity prices fixed throughout the system and move the price level, P, that is within the monetary condition $f_1(K)-g_1(P)=0$, from equilibrium. This throws the overall commodity markets out of equilibrium.

Hence a market process is set up to move P back to equilibrium, a reflection of the existence of market processes in the system that determine the price level.[23] Why, however, can the overall commodity markets come out of equilibrium?

This is because functions $f(z)$ determine only the ratios, or the relative levels, of the quantities of commodities demanded. While functions $g(z)$ determine only the ratios, or the relative levels, of the quantities of commodities supplied.

This allows the commodity markets in the aggregate to come out of equilibrium when the price level is moved from equilibrium. Then the overall excess demand (supply) of commodities that appears when P is moved from equilibrium, moves the price level back to equilibrium. Hence the price level of Model C is determinate.

However, we must go beyond this stage, which deals with an aggregative price level variable and aggregative market processes, to show that we have satisfactorily integrated the price level into the system.

This is because both this price level variable and associated market processes, on account of their aggregative character, have limited economic meaning. This is particularly because they imply that the relative prices are held fixed.

What is required is that we show that individual money prices, and hence the relative prices, are determined in the system through microeconomic market processes. This is because Model B is microeconomic in character.

To show that Model B is characterized by microeconomic market processes, let us go back to the monetary condition $f_1(K)-g_1(P)=0$ that is within (14). Next, holding the relative prices fixed, we may vary the price level P to derive a curve that shows the overall excess demand for commodities at each P.

We may then use this curve to illustrate, as we have already done, how the price level P is brought to equilibrium were it moved from equilibrium.

However, we may now go to the real or microeconomic conditions $f(z)-g(z)=0$ that are also within (14), and vary the relative prices to generate excess-demand curves that apply to individual commodity markets and hence to individual commodity prices.

Movements along these latter excess-demand curves, which will shift the position of the overall excess-demand curve

---

[23] In all our discussions concerning how prices move to equilibrium, we assume a process of *tâtonnement* and recontract.

Market Processes In The Revised Price Systems

for commodities, will bring the individual commodity markets to equilibrium to determine the individual money prices and hence the relative prices.

This reflects how we have transformed the aggregative market processes whereby the price level P was brought to equilibrium, into microeconomic market processes that determine the individual money prices and hence the relative prices. Consequently, integrating the price level into Model C required the two stages discussed.

There is a first stage that deals with an aggregative market process and an aggregative price level variable. However, this stage is simply a mathematical way-station, or a methodological device, in the process of determining microeconomic market processes and individual money prices.

This is confirmed by there being a second stage where the aggregative market process, and the aggregative price level variable of the first stage, are transformed into microeconomic market processes and individual money prices.

Hence what are determined in Model C are individual money prices, and thus the relative prices, these being determined by microeconomic market processes with money neutrality, as is appropriate for this long-run system, also being ensured.

12.5 Resolving The Invalid Neoclassical Real-Monetary Dichotomy

We shall now discuss how through the monetary Model C, we also resolve the invalid real-monetary dichotomy that characterizes Model A, a problem with the latter system that was also brought out by Patinkin.

Model C's excess-demand equations appear again below:

14. $\qquad E_j''[f_1(K) - g_1(P) = 0, f(z) - g(z) = 0] = 0$

Determining the price level of Model C required two stages. We derived the first stage from the monetary condition $f_1(K) - g_1(P) = 0$ that is within the system's excess-demand equations, namely, equations (14). Then a second stage was derived from the real or microeconomic conditions, namely, conditions $f(z) - g(z) = 0$ that are also within equations (14).

Clearly, it is the co-existence of these monetary and real or microeconomic conditions within equations (14) that brings microeconomic market processes, and hence individual money prices, into Model C.

However, the co-existence of these two conditions within equations (14) is only possible because we have resolved the hidden inconsistency of Model A, and through this, the system's invalid dichotomy.

This is because had we not resolved Model A's inconsistency through Model B, the microeconomic conditions $f(z)\text{-}g(z)\text{=}0$ in (14) of Model C would have to be replaced by those of the orthodox Model A that were set out in Chapter 3.

These are the latter system's excess demand equations, that is, equations $E_j[z]\text{=}0$ of Model A. But these orthodox conditions would conflict with the monetary condition $f_1(K)\text{-}g_1(P)\text{=}0$ in equation (14). Model C would then be transformed into Model A and an orthodox quantity theory of money equation which, as Patinkin showed, cannot be integrated in a satisfactory manner.

However, in ridding Model A of inconsistency through Model B, we replaced the orthodox microeconomic conditions $E_j[z]\text{=}0$ of Model A with the microeconomic conditions $f(z)\text{-}g(z)\text{=}0$ in (9) of Model B, our new form of the real Model A.

Next, these latter microeconomic conditions co-exist in a consistent manner with the monetary condition that is in (14) of Model C to determine the individual money prices through microeconomic market processes, while yet ensuring money neutrality.

This confirms that the co-existence of the real and monetary conditions within equations (14), and hence the determining of individual money prices through microeconomic market processes in Model C, was only possible because we have rid this latter system of the hidden inconsistency that we uncovered in Model A.

This, in turn, resolved both the latter system's price level indeterminacy and invalid dichotomy.

12.6 Review Of The New And Orthodox Price Systems

Model A, the orthodox classical system, which was formed in Chapter 3, appears below:

Model A

1. $\quad D_j \equiv F_j\left[z\right]$

2. $\quad S_j \equiv G_j\left[z\right]$

3. $\quad E_j\left[z\right]\!=\!0$

We then formed Model B below by imposing the real interior functions, functions $f(z)$ and $g(z)$, on Model A:

Model B

7. $\quad D_j \equiv F_j'\!\left[f(z)\right]$

8. $\quad S_j \equiv G_j'\!\left[g(z)\right]$

9. $\quad E_j'\!\left[f(z)\!-\!g(z)\!=\!0\right]\!=\!0$

Finally, we gave Model B a monetary form through Model C, the latter system hence being a long-run monetary system. This was through our imposing the monetary interior functions, functions $f_1(K)$ and $g_1(P)$, on Model B.

Model C then provided the basis to show that through our new approach to price systems, we resolved the issues of the price level indeterminacy and invalid real-monetary dichotomy of the orthodox neoclassical system. Model C, our long-run monetary system, appears below:

Model C

12. $\quad D_j \equiv F_j''\!\left[f_1(K), f(z)\right]$

13. $\quad S_j \equiv G_j''\!\left[g_1(P), g(z)\right]$

14. $\quad E_j''\!\left[f_1(K)\!-\!g_1(P)=0, f(z)-g(z)\!=\!0\right] = 0$

Consequently, through our new systems, we successively revised the orthodox classical system, Model A, to give the system a more general character.

12.7 Summary

We have in this book taken Model A to represent the orthodox classical system; and we focused on Keynes' criticism that the system is restricted to long-run states. Next, we resolved this problem through Model B.

This is a system which, as we discussed in Chapter 10, possesses market equilibrating processes; and these are microeconomic market processes, since Model B is microeconomic in character. However, Patinkin has shown that Model A, which he took as a neoclassical system, is subject to an invalid real-monetary dichotomy and an indeterminate price level, market processes hence being suppressed in the system.

Hence it is implied that these problems have been resolved through Model B; and we established in this chapter, through a monetary form of Model B, which is Model C, that Model B is rid of these problems.

Chapter 13

A Consistent And More General Classical System

13.1 Introduction

Through Model B, we have resolved the inconsistency we have uncovered in the orthodox classical system, Model A. This required taking, through Model B, a broader view of the classical system, compared to the orthodox view of the system through Model A.

This is reflected in a number of ways, but most generally, in Model B reflecting not only the system's long-run behavior, but also the general economic logic that should characterize all price systems.

Moreover, in this chapter, we shall examine to what extent we may look on Model B as reflecting or as being derived from the classical literature proper and the later literature on the classical and neoclassical systems. We shall find that we may indeed look on Model B as a classical system in the sense that it reflects basic elements of the orthodox classical system.

Nonetheless, the classical literature proper, and the later literature on the classical and neoclassical systems, do not bring out the key behavioral elements that provide the basis for Model B and which account for the generality of the system.

This is because this literature does not bring out how we need to incorporate into the classical system, the aspect to behavior and the associated aspect to rational behavior, that we brought into Model B.

These aspects to behavior, and the new functions that reflect this behavior, account for the greater generality of our revised classical system, Model B, compared to the orthodox form of the system, Model A.

13.2 Model B Reflects A Broader View Of the Classical Price System

Economists, in dealing with classical price theory have tended, like Keynes, to focus on the specific classical long-run system.

However, the classical price theory goes beyond this specific system. This is because while the classical economists, of course, dealt with demand and supply analysis, they did not use demand and supply functions.

Yet Model A, which is widely taken to reflect the classical system, is based on demand and supply functions. This seeming contradiction may be explained in the following manner. Demand and supply analysis has two aspects:

First, there is the general logic of this analysis which is independent of the specific forms of behavior of individual systems. Second, there is the demand (supply) analysis that is captured through the demand (supply) functions of individual systems.

These functions, of course, are intended to reflect the behavior of these individual or specific systems. However, as pointed out, the classics did not have demand and supply functions.

Hence we may assume that in not having demand (supply) functions, the classics, in their demand (supply) analysis dealt with the general logic of demand (supply) analysis, or the general logic of economic behavior. This is because this logic is independent of the behavior of specific systems.

Moreover, we shall assume that the classical system captures the general logic of demand (supply) analysis, or the general logic of economic behavior, along the lines of Model B. That is, as having a relative character, reflected in the quantities of goods that are determined in price systems being relative quantities.

This assumption is based on the analysis of Chapter 5.8 where we deduced from the classical identity form of Say's Law, that the demand (supply) analysis of Model B has a relative character. That is, in the quantities of commodities determined by the system's functions being relative quantities.

However, there is a further aspect to the classical price theory reflected in the classical system being a particular type of system, a long-run system; and the classical analysis also tells us that long-run behavior must be made to depend only on the relative prices.

Let us bring together the general logic of demand and supply analysis, or the general logic of economic behavior, as we deduced it from the classical analysis, together with the preceding property of the classical long-run system. That is, the property that the classical long-run behavior depends only on the relative prices.

This leads to a system such as Model B in that this system's functions make the relative quantities of commodities demanded (supplied) depend only on the relative prices. Hence we may look on Model B as being deduced or elicited from basic elements of classical analysis.

Clearly, however, this required taking a broader view of the classical price system. This is reflected in Model B dealing not only with the behavior of the specific classical long-run system. As well, Model B reflects the general logic of demand and supply analysis that applies across all price systems.

13.3 A Consistent And More General Classical System

We have, by drawing on our new approach to price systems, deduced or elicited a consistent system, Model B, from basic elements of the literature on the classical and neoclassical systems. This literature, as many economists have shown, is certainly not clear concerning many basic facets to classical price theory such as, for example, Say's Law and the "homogeneity postulate."[24]

However, through Model B, we captured the general logic of economic behavior or demand and supply analysis implied by the classical system's identity form of Say's Law.

Then a further aspect to the classical analysis provided for the specific long-run character of Model B's demand and supply functions. This is reflected in us making Model B's functions depend only on the relative prices.

Moreover, Model B not only reflects classical analysis in being characterized by an identity form of Say's Law and by the system's functions depending only on the relative prices. As well, Model B reflects a long-run quantity theory of money that is also associated with classical analysis.

Hence we take Model B as a classical system in the sense that it reflects or is derived from key elements of the classical analysis. However, the classical literature proper and the later literature on the classical and neoclassical systems do not bring out the key behavioral elements that account for the generality of Model B.

This is because this literature does not bring out how we need to incorporate into the classical system, the aspect to behavior, and the associated aspect to rational behavior, that we brought into Model B. It is these aspects to behavior, and the

---

[24] See, for example, Becker and Baumol, *op. cit.,* pps. 355-76.

functions that reflect this behavior, that account for the greater generality of Model B compared to the orthodox form of the classical system, Model A.

13.4 Notes On Demand And Supply Functions

We have discussed in Chapter 5.8 how Model B's long-run relative demand and supply functions may be deduced from Say's Law. However, the classical system proper is not based on demand and supply functions.

Nonetheless, when we do write such functions for the classical system, we should derive them from Say's Law. This would lead to the long-run relative demand and supply functions of Model B.

Lange, however, while forming Model A beginning with Say's Law, went on to deduce the neoclassical "homogeneity postulate" functions from the Law, Lange referring to Model A as a classical system. [25]

Whereas other economists write Model A beginning with demand and supply functions rather than Say's Law. Moreover, they use the neoclassical "homogeneity postulate" functions, functions that are not derived from Say's Law, with Model A now being referred to as a neoclassical system.

However, this neoclassical system is found to be initially inconsistent in a mathematical sense. Say's Law is then used to make the system mathematically consistent. This, however, is an invalid use of the Law which brings an incorrect form of the Law into the neoclassical Model A; and this brings the inconsistency we have uncovered into the system.

Hence the inconsistency of Model A, when taken as a neoclassical system, arose in the transition from the classical system, that is not based on demand and supply functions, to the neoclassical Model A that is based on demand and supply functions.

This transition should have been done by eliciting our relative demand and supply functions from the classical system's Say's Law, as has been done in this book, to form Model B's demand and supply functions.

This means that Model B reflects a correct identity form of the Law, since deriving Model B's functions from the Law

---

[25] O. Lange, *"Say's Law: A Restatement and Criticism,"* (1952), pps. 49-58.

requires taking the Law as a true identity. These functions then rid Model B of the inconsistency of the neoclassical Model A.

However, economists do not elicit the demand and supply functions of the neoclassical Model A from Say's Law which brings inconsistency into the system. This latter system, to review, is the form of Model A that is based on the neoclassical "homogeneity postulate" functions.

13.5 Summary

This chapter discussed how we may look on our revised classical system, Model B, as being deduced or elicited from basic elements of the classical analysis. However, this required taking a broader view, through Model B, of the classical system compared to the orthodox view of the system as reflected in Model A.

First, there is an aspect to Model B that we took as reflecting the general logic of demand and supply analysis or the general logic of economic behavior of classical price theory. This is that price systems must be given a relative character, a property we deduced from the classical identity form of Say's Law.

This is reflected in the quantities determined in Model B being relative quantities; since this ensures that the system is made consistent with limitation in resources by the behavior or economic rationale of the system.

Second, there is an aspect to the classical price system that we captured through Model B that is reflected in our making Model B's long-run behavior depend only on the relative prices. Combining these two aspects to the classical price theory led to demand and supply functions such as characterize Model B.

Hence we concluded that Model B is a classical system in the sense that it reflects basic elements of the orthodox classical system. Nonetheless, the classical literature proper, and the later literature on the classical and neoclassical systems, do not bring out the key behavioral elements that form the basis for Model B.

These, to review, are the aspect to behavior, and the associated aspect to rational behavior, that form the basis for Model B. These account for the greater generality of Model B, our revised classical system, compared to the orthodox form of the system, Model A.

Chapter 14

The Microeconomic Basis Of Macroeconomic Systems

14.1 Introduction

We have discussed how our new systems, although being microeconomic systems, yet have a macroeconomic character. However, we shall discuss in this chapter why it is possible, in the first place, for systems such as our new systems, which are microeconomic systems, to yet have a macroeconomic character.

We shall show that macroeconomic systems arise with the very formalization or systematization of the behavior of the individual and the firm in mathematical microeconomic systems. However, this formalization of behavior in microeconomic systems has to be done correctly in order to elicit the macroeconomic character of microeconomic systems.

We shall also review our condition for internal consistency of macroeconomic systems that was set out in Chapter 5.3 and how it accounts for Model B, while being a microeconomic system, yet having a macroeconomic character.

However, we shall show that this condition stems from Model B's microeconomic demand and supply functions. This confirms that Model B's macroeconomic character stems from the system's microeconomics.

14.2 Mathematical Microeconomic Price Systems

This chapter shows that macroeconomic systems arise due to the behavior of individuals and firms being captured through mathematical microeconomic price systems. But to bring out the macroeconomic element to microeconomic systems, the behavior of individuals and firms must be captured correctly through the systems.

However, as we have seen, the behavior of individuals and firms is not captured correctly through the orthodox classical system, Model A. This, to review, is because this system's functions do not reflect behavior that is consistent with limitation in resources. This, in turn, results in Model A's macroeconomic character being suppressed.

On the other hand, the behavior of individuals and firms is correctly captured in Model B, our revised classical system, through the latter system's demand and supply functions; since the functions reflect behavior that is consistent with limitation in resources.

This, as we shall now discuss, accounts for our new systems, while being microeconomic systems, yet having a macroeconomic character.

14.3 Macroeconomic Systems Arise Out Of Mathematical Microeconomic Systems

There is an economic inconsistency in the orthodox form of the classical system, Model A, that results in the system being restricted to long-run states. This inconsistency arises because the system's functions do not reflect behavior that is consistent with limitation in resources.

This economic inconsistency, in turn, leads to Model A being initially inconsistent in a mathematical sense. Then Say's Law is imposed on the system to make it mathematically consistent; and this is generally taken to mean that the system is indeed consistent.

However, Model A remains inconsistent in an economic sense; since the system's economic inconsistency can only be satisfactorily resolved by revising the system's economic rationale through revising the system's demand and supply functions.

Moreover, not only does Model A remain inconsistent in an economic sense. As well, the system's inconsistency is given an additional form. This is because Model A is made mathematically through Say's Law being imposed on the system; and this transforms the Law into an incorrect form. This incorrect Say's Law, in turn, restricts the system to long-run states.

This restriction of the system to long-run states is the additional form that Model A's initial economic inconsistency now takes, an inconsistency that stems from the system's demand and supply functions and hence from the system's microeconomics.

However, through Model B, we resolved the inconsistency in Model A's microeconomics. This was through our revising the latter system's demand and supply functions, through Model B's functions, to make them reflect behavior that is consistent with limitation in resources.

This, in turn, led to Model B being automatically consistent in a mathematical sense. This meant that we did not need to use Say's Law, as in Model A, to make Model B mathematically consistent. This was a use of the Law in Model A that brought an incorrect form of the Law into the latter system that restricts the system to long-run states.

Hence our not having to use the Law to make Model B mathematically consistent led to Model B being characterized by a correct form of the Law, a form of the Law which, as we showed in Chapter 9, cannot restrict Model B to long-run states.

This means that Model A's *microeconomic inconsistency,* which arises from the hidden inconsistency in the system, results in the Law being transformed into an incorrect form, a form that restricts the system to long-run states.

Consequently, we find the system's microeconomic inconsistency to be also reflected in the system being restricted to long-run states, the system hence also now reflecting a *macroeconomic inconsistency.*

On the other hand, Model B's *microeconomic consistency,* resulting from this system resolving the hidden inconsistency of Model A, brings a correct form of the Law into Model B, a form of the Law that cannot possibly restrict the latter system to long-run states.

Hence Model B's microeconomic consistency results in the system being able to move into alternative states, the system hence also being consistent in a *macroeconomic* sense.

14.4 The Keynesian And The New Approach To The Classical System

Model A's demand and supply functions do not ensure that the system is consistent with limitation in resources. Whereas Model B's demand and supply functions ensure that the system is consistent with limitation in resources. Hence Model A reflects a restricted approach to microeconomics compared to Model B.

However, on this basis alone, we could not fully see why Model A is indeed inconsistent while Model B is consistent. This is because Model A seems to be a consistent system, particularly because it is consistent in a mathematical sense; and the system has long been taken for this reason as being consistent.

What was also required to fully judge consistency of Model A was to also judge the system *as a macroeconomic system;* and Keynes did find that Model A, which we are using to represent the orthodox classical system, lacks a macroeconomic character in being restricted to long-run states by Say's Law.

We may now readily see how our approach to the classical system differs from Keynes' approach to the system. Keynes, finding that the classical system is restricted to long-run states, proceeded to form a macroeconomic system that can describe short-run states which is not possible with the classical system.

As a result, Keynes' system is an alternative to the classical system, the Keynesian and classical systems hence being dichotomized. This is confirmed by Keynes leaving the classical system untouched and hence still characterized by the problem of being restricted to long-run states and by the incorrect form of Say's Law that causes this.

However, we found an economic inconsistency within Model A. This, to review, arises because Model A's functions do not reflect behavior that is consistent with limitation in resources.

We then resolved this inconsistency through Model B to bring a more general approach to the behavior of individuals and firms, and hence to microeconomics, into the latter system. Then we found that Model B is not necessarily restricted to long-run states but can move into other states were behavior to change.

This gives Model B a macroeconomic character yet the system is a microeconomic system in being based wholly on the behavior of the individual and the firm. This analysis brings out how restricted is the orthodox approach to price systems compared to our new approach.

This new approach leads to systems, as illustrated by Model B, that are simultaneously both microeconomic and macroeconomic in character, the approach hence integrating microeconomic and macroeconomic systems. Whereas the orthodox approach leads to systems that are *either* microeconomic, like Model A, *or* macroeconomic, like the Keynesian system, systems that are hence dichotomized.

14.5 Basing Macroeconomic Systems On Microeconomic Behavior

Let us draw on the earlier analysis of Chapter 5.3 to show how we may form macroeconomic systems from microeconomic analysis. This requires a more general approach to microeconomics compared to the orthodox approach; and we arrived at this more general microeconomics through resolving the inconsistency we uncovered in Model A through Model B.

This explained why Model B is based on a more general approach to microeconomics compared to Model A; and this provided the basis whereby Model B, while being a microeconomic system, could be given a macroeconomic character. This required drawing on the condition for internal consistency of macroeconomic systems set out earlier in the book

To review, we discussed in Chapter 5.3 how, to form a macroeconomic system, we must first rid our system of the incorrect form of Say's Law of Model A that restricts the latter system to long-run states. Hence our system, in principle, can move beyond long-run states.

However, there must also be an actual means whereby the system is made to move to alternative states. This is ensured by the system being characterized by a behaviorally-determined overall output or income variable.

Next, as also discussed in Chapter 5.3. the means whereby the system is made, in principle, able to move to alternative states, must necessarily be consistent with the system's overall output or income variable to ensure internal consistency of the system.

This is the case with the Keynesian system; but both the means whereby the Keynesian system is rid of Model A's Say's Law and the Keynesian system's overall output or income variable, are macroeconomic in character. This results in the microeconomics of the real part of the Keynesian system being suppressed.

On the other hand, we rid Model B of Model A's incorrect form of Say's Law through the more general microeconomics that characterizes Model B. Moreover, Model B also had to be characterized by a behaviorally-determined overall output or income variable.

This would ensure that the system has an actual means whereby it is made to move to alternative states as behavior changes. This overall output or income also had to be consistent with Model B's microeconomic character to ensure internal consistency of the system; and such consistency was ensured.

This was through Model B's overall output or income variable W also taking on the meaning of a budget constraint. This made it consistent with Model B's microeconomic character; since this budget constraint provided the basis for the maximizing behavior of the individual and the firm.

Hence Model B has a macroeconomic character in being able to move to alternative states as behavior changes. Yet the system is a microeconomic system in being based wholly on the behavior of the individual and the firm,

14.6 The Microeconomic Basis Of Macroeconomic Systems

We discussed earlier how Model B meets our general condition for internal consistency of macroeconomic systems. This condition, to review, required that the overall output or income variable of Model B, which reflects the system's macroeconomic character, also reflect the system's budget constraint; since this made the system's macroeconomic character consistent with the system being a microeconomic system.

This is a very general approach to establishing that Model B, which is a microeconomic system, yet has a macroeconomic character. However, we shall now establish this by showing how this general condition for internal consistency of macroeconomic systems stems from Model B's microeconomic demand and supply functions.

We showed in Chapter 6.7 that the variable W, that reflects Model B's overall output or income, is brought into the behavioral content of the system by the system's internal functions. This, in turn, transforms W to also reflect the system's limited resources or budget constraint.

Moreover, the movement of W into the behavioral content of Model B, as was also discussed in Chapter 6.7, rids the system of Model A's incorrect form of Say's Law that restricts the latter system to long-run states. Hence Model B is not restricted in this way.

Consequently, Model B will move to alternative states as behavior changes, the system hence having a macroeconomic character. As a result, Model B's microeconomic functions are consistent with our general condition for internal consistency of macroeconomic systems.

This confirms that macroeconomic systems arise out of consistent mathematical microeconomic systems; since we were only able to elicit the macroeconomic character of Model B because we correctly capture the behavior of the individual and the firm in this system.

By the same token, Model A's macroeconomic character is suppressed because the behavior of the individual and the firm is not captured correctly in this system.

Thus Model A, to review, is initially inconsistent in a mathematical sense. Say's Law is then imposed on the system to make it mathematically consistent. This imposes on Model A, the variable W that reflects the system's overall output or income.

However, this variable remains outside the behavioral content of Model A hence it cannot be brought into the system's behavioral content as a budget constraint as in Model B. Hence Model A remains characterized by an incorrect form of Say's Law that restricts the system to long-run states.

Clearly, these problems arise because Model A's functions, in not correctly reflecting the behavior of the individual and the firm, are inconsistent with our general condition for internal consistency of macroeconomic systems. This explains why Model A's macroeconomic character is suppressed.

14.7 Summary

We discussed in this chapter why it is possible for our new systems, which are wholly microeconomic systems, to yet have a macroeconomic character; and we found that the very systematization of economic behavior, meaning the behavior of the individual and the firm, in mathematical microeconomic price systems, leads to systems that have a macroeconomic character.

Now to elicit the macroeconomic character of mathematical microeconomic systems, the systematization of economic behavior through these systems has to be done correctly.

However, this was not the case with the orthodox classical system, Model A, on account of the inconsistency we have uncovered in the system; and this suppressed the system's macroeconomic character which resulted in the system being restricted to long-run states.

On the other hand, the behavior of the individual and the firm is correctly systematized in Model B, our revised classical system. This gives the system a consistent microeconomic character; and this led to our eliciting a macroeconomic character from the microeconomic Model B.

Consequently, the very systematization of economic behavior through Model B results in the system, while being a microeconomic system, yet having a macroeconomic character.

Finally, we reviewed our condition for internal consistency of macroeconomic systems that was set out in Chapter 5.3. Both the Keynesian system and Model B meet this condition hence both systems are internally consistent macroeconomic systems.

However, Model B, while having a macroeconomic character, is a microeconomic system, in being based wholly on the behavior of the individual and the firm. This is because while Model B is a microeconomic system, the system meets our general condition for internal consistency of macroeconomic systems.

This leads to Model B's overall output or income variable, which reflects the system's macroeconomic character, being made to reflect the system's budget constraint. This budget constraint, in turn, provides the basis for the maximizing behavior of the individual and the firm which makes it consistent with the system's microeconomic character.

This reflects how Model B's macroeconomic character is consistent with the system being a wholly microeconomic system; and this confirms that macroeconomic systems arise with the very formalizing of the behavior of the individual and the firm in consistent mathematical microeconomic systems.

Chapter 15

The Economics And Mathematics Of Price Systems

15.1 Introduction

There is a basic theme running through the book which is that our new systems, which we represented by Model B, are based wholly on economic principles or economic behavior. This is because there is no interference with these principles or behavior stemming from mathematical elements of the systems.

Mathematical elements, of course, characterize our new systems but they are not a part of the economic substance of the systems. This is because the mathematics of our new systems is solely a vehicle for the systems' economics. This accounts for the generality of our new systems.

Whereas the behavior or economic rationale of orthodox systems such as Model A is restricted by mathematical elements; and this limits the generality of the systems.

15.2 Mathematical And Economic Consistency Of Price Systems

We have shown that the general economic rationale or behavior of our new systems, which we represent by Model B, is not restricted by mathematical elements. This is because mathematical consistency of the systems stems from the systems' economic rationale.

This is a result of our new demand and supply functions of Model B reflecting an aspect to behavior that is missing from the orthodox-type functions. This, in turn, elicited a consistent mathematical approach in Model B since our mathematics was simply a vehicle for the system's consistent economic rationale.

This resulted in Model B being automatically consistent in a mathematical sense. On the other hand, there is an inconsistent general economic rationale underlying the orthodox classical system, Model A; since, as we have discussed, there is an aspect to the behavior of individuals and firms that is missing from the latter system.

142

Namely, the aspect to behavior that should ensure that the system is consistent with limitation in resources. This, in turn, causes Model A to be initially inconsistent in a mathematical sense.

Next, Model A is made mathematically consistent; and this ensures that the system is consistent with limitation in resources. Hence Model A's mathematics becomes a substitute for the aspect to behavior that should ensure that the system is consistent with limitation in resources, which is an incorrect use of mathematics.

15.3 Remarks On The Orthodox And New Systems

There is an economic inconsistency in Model A because the behavior in the system, and hence the system's demand and supply functions, do not ensure that the system is consistent with limitation in resources.

This, in turn, causes Model A to be initially inconsistent in a mathematical sense. Say's Law is then imposed on the system to eliminate a surplus equation, to make the system mathematically consistent; and this, as we have shown, ensures that the system is consistent with limitation in resources.

This, however, reflects an attempt to make a system that is inconsistent in an economic sense, consistent by making it consistent in a mathematical sense, which is impossible. Hence as would be expected, an economic inconsistency remains in Model A but this inconsistency is given an additional form.

This results in Say's Law being transformed into an incorrect form that restricts the system to long-run states. This is the additional form Model A's initial economic inconsistency, that characterizes the system's demand and supply functions, now takes.

Hence Model A had to be revised to resolve the problem of the system being restricted to long-run states. This required removing the underlying cause of the system's inconsistency. This, to review, is an inconsistency that arises because Model A's functions do not reflect behavior that is consistent with limitation in resources.

Consequently, we had to revise Model A's demand and supply functions to transform them into those of Model B, functions that reflect behavior that is consistent with limitation in resources; and through Model B, we resolved the inconsistency of Model A and the problem of the restriction of the latter system to long-run states.

Keynes, however, finding that Model A is restricted to long-run states, proceeded to form his macroeconomic system by removing from his system, Model A's Say's Law that restricts this latter system to long-run states. Hence Keynes' macroeconomic system describes short-run states. But his system is an alternative to Model A hence it is dichotomized from Model A.

However, we found an economic inconsistency *within* Model A that arises because the system's functions do not reflect behavior that is consistent with limitation in resources.

This led, in Chapter 5, to our finding our new type of demand and supply functions that formed the basis of Model B; and through the latter system, we resolved Model A's economic inconsistency. This, in turn, resolved the problem of Model A being restricted to long-run states.

This is because, as was discussed in Chapter 6.4, Model B is automatically consistent in a mathematical sense. Hence we did not need Say's Law to make this latter system consistent. This resulted in Model B being characterized by a correct form of Say's Law.

This is a form of the Law which, as we confirmed in Chapter 9, is a true identity that hence cannot possibly restrict Model B to long-run states or indeed restrict the system in any other way.

15.4 Model B Is Wholly Behavioral In Character

We may readily show that Model B, our revised classical system, is wholly behavioral in character. First, we show Model A below:

Model A

1. $D_j \equiv F_j[z]$

2. $S_j \equiv G_j[z]$

3. $E_j[z] = 0$

As well, we show below the Say's Law identity below:

4. $ad \equiv as$

We have discussed how Model A is initially inconsistent in a mathematical sense. Then the Say's Law identity is imposed on the system to eliminate a surplus equation to make the system mathematically consistent.

This reflects a misuse of mathematics; since Say's Law is an identity or truism hence it should not be given a substantive role in a system. However, it is made to act as an external budget constraint to ensure mathematical consistency of Model A.

This brings an incorrect form of Say's Law into the system that restricts it to long-run states. Let us review how this has been resolved through Model B" which is shown below. However, we shall now simply refer to Model B" in our discussion as Model B since the two systems are interchangeable:

Model B"

7". $D_j \equiv F_j'[W, f(z)]$

8". $S_j \equiv G_j'[W, g(z)]$

9". $E_j'[W, f(z) - g(z) = 0] = 0$

We formed the variable W in Chapter 5.4 by collapsing the aggregate demand and supply variables in the Say's Law identity into the single variable W. This variable reflects the overall output or income as well as the limited resources of both Model A and Model B".

However, W is a long-run output or income and in being imposed on Model A from the outside, it restricts the system to long-run states.

Clearly, also, Say's Law, in being reduced to the variable W, cannot now be used to ensure that Model A is mathematically consistent. However, this has been resolved through Model B. This is because, as we showed in Chapter 6.4, Model B is automatically consistent in a mathematical sense.

Hence we do not need to impose Say's Law on Model B to make this system mathematically consistent; and this rids Model B of Model A's incorrect form of the Law that restricts the latter system to long-run states. This is because of the new aspect to behavior we brought into Model B.

We may now readily show that Model B is wholly behavioral in character.

This, of course, is already implied by Model B being automatically consistent in a mathematical sense; since this means that the mathematics of Model B cannot restrict the system's behavior or economic rationale. Let us, however, illustrate this in more detail.

As discussed, we elicit the variable W from Say's Law, a variable that reflects the overall output of both Model A and Model B. Next, this same variable that we elicit from Say's Law enters the demand and supply functions of Model B.

This gives the W in Model B the additional meaning of reflecting the system's limited resources or budget constraint. This is reflected in the internal functions of Model B, functions $f(z)$ and $g(z)$, operating respectively on W to determine the quantities of commodities demanded and supplied.

Hence taking it that individuals and firms maximize their utility and profit subject to a budget constraint, we must assume that the quantities determined in Model B by functions $f(z)$ and $g(z)$ operating on W are a consequence of this maximizing behavior.

Moreover, we have shown that the budget constraint W of Model B itself arises on account of the rational behavior of individuals and firms in the system. Consequently, Model B is wholly behavioral in character.

15.5 Summary

We discussed in this chapter how price systems formed using our new approach to the systems are based wholly on economic principles or behavior. This is because there is no interference with these principles or behavior stemming from mathematical elements in the systems.

This is reflected in our new systems being automatically consistent in a mathematical sense. As a result, the systems' mathematics cannot possibly restrict the systems' economics. Nonetheless, mathematical elements characterize our new systems but they are not a part of the economic substance of the systems.

This is because the mathematics of our new systems is solely a vehicle for the systems' economics. This accounts for the generality of our new systems compared to orthodox systems such as Model A; since the behavior or economic rationale of Model A is restricted by mathematical elements which limits the generality of the latter system.

Chapter 16

Generality Of The New Approach To Price Systems

16.1 Introduction

Through resolving the inconsistency we have uncovered in the orthodox classical system, we came upon a more general approach to microeconomics; and this chapter will go into further detail concerning how this new approach to microeconomics accounts for us integrating microeconomic and macroeconomic systems.

This, to review, is because our more general approach to microeconomics brings a unity to price systems in terms of their general economic logic. On the other hand, orthodox microeconomic and macroeconomic systems, in lacking this more general approach to microeconomics, are dichotomized.

This, we shall find, is reflected in their being a restricted use of the concept of overall output or income in these microeconomic and macroeconomic systems. However, this restriction is removed through our more general approach to microeconomics that characterizes Model B.

16.2 Generalizing Model A Through Model B

There are discussions in the classical literature of economic behavior or demand and supply analysis; and we concluded earlier that such discussions, in not being based on demand and supply functions, dealt with the general logic of demand and supply analysis or the general logic of economic behavior.

Moreover, the classical Say's Law led us to conclude, as we discussed in Chapter 5.8, that the general logic of demand (supply) analysis, or the general logic of economic behavior, is reflected in this logic having an innate relative character.

That is, in the quantities of commodities demanded and supplied being relative quantities demanded and relative quantities supplied; since this will result in these quantities adjusting in a relative manner so as to always sum to a limited volume of resources. This ensures that price systems are consistent with limitation in resources.

Hence to capture the general logic of demand and supply analysis, or the general logic of economic behavior, we must take quantities as being relative quantities.

This means that when we write specific price systems using demand and supply functions, we must ensure that these functions, although applying to specific systems, also reflect the general logic of demand and supply analysis or the general logic of economic behavior.

Consequently, we must ensure that demand and supply functions, as illustrated by those of Model B, have an innate relative character reflected in the functions determining relative quantities.

However, the orthodox-type functions such as stem from neoclassical analysis, as illustrated by Model A's functions, do not have such an innate relative character. This led to Model A's macroeconomic character, that should have emerged with the systematization of economic behavior through this system, being suppressed.

This, in turn, became reflected in the system being restricted to long-run states by an incorrect form of Say's Law.

Keynes then proceeded to form his macroeconomic system to resolve this problem with the classical system; but the Keynesian system is an alternative to the classical, the systems hence being dichotomized. Moreover, the Keynesian system does not have a satisfactory basis in microeconomics.

However, we revised Model A, through Model B, to correctly capture the general logic of demand and supply analysis or the general logic of economic behavior. This was through framing Model B's demand and supply functions to have an innate relative character.

This, as we showed in Chapter 6, rid Model B of an incorrect form of Say's Law of Model A that restricts the latter system to long-run states. This incorrect Law, as was discussed in Chapter 9, was then replaced in Model B by a correct form of the Law, a form of the Law which, in being a true identity, cannot restrict Model B to long-run states.

Hence Model B can move into short-run states were behavior to change; and this gives the system a macroeconomic character even though it is a microeconomic system in being based wholly on the behavior of the individual and the firm. As a result, Model B's macroeconomic character emerged as a result of our basing the system on a more general approach to microeconomics compared to the orthodox approach.

16.3 Why The Keynesian System Does Not Have A Satisfactory Basis In Microeconomics

Model B, as we have shown, is rid of Model A's incorrect form of Say's Law that restricts the latter system to long-run states. Hence Model B, although being a microeconomic system, can move to short-run states were behavior to change, the system hence having a macroeconomic character.

This means that like the Keynesian system, overall output W is also behaviorally determined in Model B, a reflection of both systems having a macroeconomic character. Yet Model B, unlike the Keynesian system, is a wholly microeconomic system.

Let us discuss the reason for this difference between the systems. Model B" is shown again below but we shall simply refer to it as Model B since the two systems are interchangeable:

Model B"

7". $\quad D_j \equiv F'_j[W, f(z)]$

8". $\quad S_j \equiv G'_j[W, g(z)]$

9". $\quad E'_j[W, f(z) - g(z) = 0] = 0$

We have represented the behaviorally-determined overall output or income of both the Keynesian system and Model B by the variable W. However, the rationale underlying the W of Model B differs significantly from the rationale underlying the W of the Keynesian system.

We have discussed how the W of the Keynesian system abstracts from or suppresses the microeconomics of the real part of the Keynesian system. This results in the individual quantities of commodities and the commodity relative prices being suppressed.

This, moreover, is confirmed by the Keynesian W directly entering the markets of the Keynesian system where it is determined by aggregate demand and supply functions; but these functions suppress the microeconomics of the real part of the Keynesian system.

However, the overall output variable W of Model B does not suppress the system's microeconomics. This is because W enters the system as a budget constraint in entering the system's demand and supply functions, functions (7") and (8"). Next,

Model B's interior functions $f(z)$ and $g(z)$ operate on W to determine the individual quantities of commodities demanded and supplied.

These individual quantities of commodities then enter the markets of the system, reflecting how Model B is a microeconomic system. This is because it is based wholly on the behavior of the individual and the firm. Yet Model B, as we have discussed, can move to alternative states as behavior changes, the system hence also having a macroeconomic character.

16.4 Giving The Keynesian System A Satisfactory Microeconomic Character

To review, both the Keynesian system and Model B can move to alternative states where various W, that is, various levels of overall output or income, are determined by the behavior or market processes of the systems; and this gives the systems a macroeconomic character.

However, the variable W of Model B not only reflects the system's overall output or income. As well, it also simultaneously reflects the system's limited resources or budget constraint.

Moreover, we also discussed in Chapter 6.7 how the interior functions $f(z)$ and $g(z)$ of Model B bring the system's limited resources or budget constraint, W, into the behavioral content of the system. These same functions then operate on W to determine the individual quantities of commodities demanded and supplied. This reflects how Model B is microeconomic in character.

However, the Keynesian system is not based on such microeconomic analysis. This is because the system lacks functions that have the relative form of $f(z)$ and $g(z)$ of Model B. These functions in Model B reflect how individuals and firms are aware that their resources are limited and hence they act in light of this awareness.

Moreover, individuals and firms in Model B are made aware that their resources are limited by W being brought into the system's demand and supply functions by functions $f(z)$ and $g(z)$ These same functions then operate on W to determine the individual quantities of commodities demanded and supplied. Let us now consider the Keynesian system.

This system determines various levels of overall output, that is, various W. However, these different W of the Keynesian system cannot be brought as budget constraints, of relevance to microeconomics, into the behavioral content of the Keynesian system as in Model B.

This is because the Keynesian system lacks functions with the relative form of functions $f(z)$ and $g(z)$ that characterize Model B. As a result, the Keynesian system lacks the aspect to behavior, and associated rational behavior, that these functions bring into Model B. Hence to give the Keynesian system a satisfactory microeconomic character, we must bring this aspect to behavior into the system.

This, to review, is the aspect to behavior reflected in us taking individuals and firms to be aware that their resources are limited and hence they act in light of this awareness. Let us discuss how this is to be done.

To review, the Keynesian system determines different volumes of overall output, that is, different W, in the various states that the system may describe. These Keynesian W, however, as we discussed in Chapter 11.4, do not stem from the behavior of the individual and the firm. This explains why they suppress the microeconomics of the real part of the Keynesian system.

Hence to give the Keynesian system a satisfactory microeconomic character, we must transform the Keynesian W to make them stem from the behavior of the individual and the firm. This is accomplished by bringing into the Keynesian system, the new aspect to the behavior of individuals and firms, and the associated rational behavior, that characterize Model B.

Consequently, we must base the Keynesian system on Model B's type of demand and supply functions, to hence give the Keynesian system a satisfactory microeconomic character. This will transform the Keynesian W to make them stem from the behavior of the individual and the firm.

This is because the Keynesian system will now reflect the aspect to rational behavior that characterizes Model B. This rational behavior, as we have discussed in connection with Model B, is reflected in individuals and firms determining their commodity demands and supplies in the knowledge or awareness that their resources are limited.

This will give utility to the Keynesian W hence these W will enter the behavioral content of the revised Keynesian system to replace the W of the initial Keynesian system. Moreover, these new Keynesian W will not reflect only the overall output or income of the transformed Keynesian system; as well, they will reflect the system's limited resources or budget constraint.

Hence the revised Keynesian system will be macroeconomic in character like the Keynesian system proper, in being characterized by the variable W. However, this variable is quite different from the W of the initial Keynesian system.

This is because the W of the revised Keynesian system stems from the behavior of the individual and the firm. Whereas this is not the case with the W of the original Keynesian system. This may be confirmed in the following way.

We have discussed earlier how the initial Keynesian W suppresses the microeconomics of the real part of the Keynesian system. This is a reflection of how this Keynesian W does not stem from the behavior of the individual and the firm.

On the other hand, the W of the revised Keynesian systems enters the system as a budget constraint. Next, following Model B, internal functions operate on this W to determine individual quantities of commodities demanded and supplied.

Hence the W of the revised Keynesian system is consistent with the microeconomic character that now characterizes the system. This is a reflection of how the W of the revised Keynesian system stems from the behavior of the individual and the firm. As a result, the revised Keynesian system, unlike the Keynesian system proper, is wholly microeconomic in character.

Clearly, the general logic of the Keynesian system has to be significantly transformed in order to give the system a satisfactory microeconomic character.

To review, as was discussed in Chapter 11.4, the Keynesian W does not stem from the behavior of the individual and the firm; and it suppresses the microeconomic character of the real part of the Keynesian system.

However, we have now transformed the Keynesian W into the W of Model B that stem from the behavior of the individual and the firm as was also discussed in Chapter 11.4; and these latter W do not suppress the microeconomic character of the real part of the transformed Keynesian system.

Moreover, the Keynesian aggregate demand and supply functions disappear from the transformed Keynesian system. This is because the overall output variable W in the transformed Keynesian system is not now a market-determined variable.

This results in the Keynesian aggregate demand and supply functions, that determine W in the initial Keynesian system, becoming redundant in our transformed Keynesian system, a reflection of the system now being wholly microeconomic in character.

16.5 Generalizing Microeconomic And Macroeconomic Systems

We have discussed how through our new approach to price systems, we gave the orthodox classical microeconomic system, a macroeconomic character. Moreover, we also discussed how through this new approach to price systems we may also give the Keynesian macroeconomic system a satisfactory microeconomic character.

Hence we integrated microeconomic and macroeconomic systems from the perspective of both the microeconomic classical system and the macroeconomic Keynesian system.

This was possible because our new approach to price systems reflects a more general approach to microeconomics compared to the orthodox approach; and we may look on this as resulting from our new approach to microeconomics removing a restriction on a key variable in orthodox price systems. This is the overall output or income variable.

Now the overall output or income variable allows us to view price systems in overall or macroeconomic terms. However, there is a basic problem in orthodox price theory concerning how this variable is integrated into formal or mathematical price systems.

This is because once we deal with an aggregative or macroeconomic overall output or income variable in price systems, we need to give it the broader meaning discussed in this book. That is, we must also give this overall output or income variable the additional meaning of a budget or income constraint; since unless this is done, we restrict the generality of our systems.

Let us illustrate this by first considering the orthodox classical system, Model A, then we shall consider the Keynesian system. An overall output or income variable does not appear explicitly in Model A. However, we were able to elicit such a variable from Say's Law that is imposed on the system to make it mathematically consistent.

This, as was discussed in Chapter 5.4, was by our collapsing the aggregate demand and supply variables in the Say's Law identity to form the single overall output or income variable that we denoted by W.

Next, this variable is imposed on Model A by Say's Law; and since this W is a long-run overall output variable, it restricts the system to long-run states. This reflects how the overall output variable W restricts Model A's microeconomics to long-run states. Let us discuss how this was resolved.

We discussed in Chapter 6.7 how the variable W is moved from outside the behavioral content of Model A into the behavioral content of Model B. Hence we retained the overall output or income concept in Model B that is reflected in W. However, we also gave W the meaning of a budget constraint in the latter system; since W also took on the meaning of a budget constraint when it moved into the behavioral content of Model B.

This, through Model B, removed the restriction on the generality of Model A's microeconomics we have discussed; since Model B, on account of the movement of W into the system's behavioral content, was thereby rid of Model A's incorrect Say's Law that restricts the latter system to long-run states as we discussed in Chapter 6.7.

This meant that Model B could move to alternative states as behavior changes, the system hence being characterized by a microeconomics that is not restricted to long-run states but applies in all states that Model B may describe. Whereas, as we discussed earlier, Model A's microeconomics is restricted to long-run states

Hence while we may use the overall output or income variable in price systems, we must also give it the meaning of reflecting the systems' limited resources or budget constraints. Clearly, it is because the W of Model A is not given this broader meaning that the microeconomics of the system is restricted in the manner described.

Moreover, this problem also characterizes the Keynesian system and also restricts the system's microeconomics. This is because Keynes took W in the narrow sense of reflecting only the overall output or income of his system. This, as we have shown, suppresses the microeconomics of the real part of the Keynesian system.

However, as discussed in the previous section we may, through Model B, give the Keynesian W the broader meaning of also reflecting the limited resources or budget constraint of the system. We thereby resolve, through Model B, the restriction of the microeconomics of the real part of the Keynesian system.

16.6 Remarks On Integrating Microeconomic And Macroeconomic Systems

We discussed in Section 16.2 of the chapter how we may, through our new approach to price systems, generalize orthodox *microeconomic* systems such as Model A, through Model B, to give the systems a *macroeconomic* character.

Moreover, we also discussed in Section 16.4 how through this new approach to price systems, we may generalize the Keynesian *macroeconomic* system to give the system a satisfactory *microeconomic* character.

We may look on this generalizing of Model A and the Keynesian system as a result of our imposing on both systems, the more general approach to rational behavior of Model B.

This rational behavior, to review, reflects how individuals and firms, acting rationally, demand and supply commodities in the knowledge or awareness that their resources are limited. This gives utility to individuals and firms of a variable that reflects their overall resources or budget constraint.

This, in turn, gives rise to the variable W which, while reflecting the overall output or income of our new systems, also reflects the limited resources or budget constraint of individuals and firms. Moreover, this budget constraint W arises in whatever state the new systems may describe.

Internal functions that characterize our new systems then operate on the current W to determine the individual quantities of commodities demanded and supplied. Hence all of our new systems are based on microeconomic behavior; since this process exists in all of the systems.

This, to review, is because in all of these new systems, the rational behavior of individuals and firms leads to the emergence of budget constraints such as W in whatever states the systems may describe, states determined by the macroeconomic behavior of the systems.

These budget constraints, in turn, provide the basis for the maximizing behavior of the individual and the firm. Hence all of our new systems emerge out of our more general approach to microeconomic analysis; and this integrates the systems.

16.7 Summary

Through resolving the inconsistency we have uncovered in the orthodox classical system, we came upon a more general approach to microeconomics; and we focused in this chapter on how this more general approach to microeconomics accounts for us integrating microeconomic and macroeconomic systems. This is by bringing a unity to the systems in terms of their general economic logic.

This was illustrated by our showing how through our more general approach to microeconomics, we may give the orthodox classical microeconomic system, Model A, a macroeconomic character. Moreover, through this more general microeconomics, we may also give the Keynesian macroeconomic system, a satisfactory microeconomic character.

This chapter also brought out how there is a restricted use of the concept of overall output or income in both Model A and the Keynesian system. However, this restriction is removed through our more general approach to microeconomics that characterizes Model B.

Chapter 17

Issues Concerning Say's Law

17.1 Introduction

Keynes held in his *General Theory* that the classical system is restricted by Say's Law to describing long-run, full-employment states. On the other hand, Keynes' system can describe short-run states that are characterized by general unemployment.

Hence Keynes concluded that his system is more general than the classical system in that the latter system is restricted to describing only long-run, full-employment states. This led to lengthy controversies about the classical and Keynesian systems; and this chapter covers some of the issues raised in the controversies particularly within the context of Say's Law.

Finally, we shall discuss how the issue of Say's Law was resolved through the approach to rational behavior that characterizes Model B, our revised classical system.

17.2 The Identity Nature Of Say's Law

Central to many controversies about the classical system is the issue of Say's Law; and controversy about the Law centered on the Law being an identity which, according to Keynes, restricts the classical system to long-run states.

Other economists have also shown that the Law invalidly dichotomizes the orthodox classical system, Model A, into real and monetary parts and mars the system in other ways. Hence the Law seemed so problematic that many economists attempted to show that it is not an identity or that it is not a part of the classical system.

However, the issue of the Law could not be settled on the basis of whether or not it is an identity or whether or not it is a part of the classical system. Let us discuss the first of these issues here with the other being covered in Section 17.4 below.

We shall find that the issue of Say's Law could not be settled on the basis of whether or not the Law is an identity because the Law is an identity in both Model A and Model B. Yet there is an incorrect form of the Law in Model A but a correct form of the Law in Model B. Let us first show that the Law is indeed an identity in both Model A and Model B.

We discussed in Chapter 9 how the relative character of Model B's functions, reflected in the functions determining relative quantities of commodities, allows us to describe W, which reflects the overall output or income of the system, alternately as aggregate demand and aggregate supply.

Hence Model B's functions brought a true identity form of the Law into the system. That is, a form of the Law that is solely a descriptive device.

Next, we discussed in Chapter 5 how the quantities in Model A are transformed into relative quantities, as a result of the system being made mathematically consistent. This, in turn, brings an identity form of Say's Law into Model A just as the relative character of Model B's functions brought an identity form of the Law into that system.

Consequently, Say's Law is an identity in both Model A and Model B. Yet as we shall now discuss, there is an incorrect form of the Law in Model A but a correct form of the Law in Model B.

17.3 Incorrect And Correct Forms Of Say's Law

We shall find that there is an incorrect form of Say's Law in Model A because the Law in this system is associated with or mirrors the inconsistency of the system. Whereas there is a correct form of the Law in Model B because the Law in this system is associated with or mirrors the consistency of the system. Let us first consider Model A.

This system's functions are inconsistent in an economic sense because they do not ensure that the system is consistent with limitation in resources. This is because the functions lack the aspect to behavior that ensures that a system is consistent with limitation in resources.

This, in turn, causes Model A to be initially inconsistent in a mathematical sense.

Say's Law is then imposed on Model A to make the system mathematically consistent; and this ensures that the system is consistent with limitation in resources. This, however, transforms the Law into an incorrect form that restricts the system to long-run states.

This is because the Law is given the invalid role of ensuring that the system is consistent with limitation in resources, a role that should be performed by the system's demand and supply functions.

As a result, there is an incorrect form of Say's Law in Model A that traces to an inconsistency in the behavior underlying the system. Let us now consider Model B.

This system's functions are consistent since the functions ensure that the system is consistent with limitation in resources. Hence the functions reflect the aspect to behavior that is missing from Model A. This, in turn, ensures that Model B is automatically consistent in a mathematical sense.

As a result, Say's Law in Model B is relieved of the incorrect role forced on it in Model A of making the latter system consistent with limitation in resources through making the system mathematically consistent; and this led to Model B being characterized by a correct form of the Law that reflects or mirrors the consistency of the system.

17.4 There Is A Correct Form Of Say's Law In The Revised Classical System

We shall now discuss the second issue referred to in Section 17.2 above. This is whether the issue of Say's Law could be settled on the grounds of whether or not the Law is a part of the classical system; and it will be found that the Law is indeed a part of the classical system.

However, to show this first requires forming a consistent classical system such as Model B. Then within this classical system, we find a correct form of Say's Law. This is a form of the Law that is a true identity which hence cannot have any substantive influence in Model B. Let us discuss this.

Economists, in discussing the issue of Say's Law, generally focused on Model A since this system is widely taken to represent the classical system.

However, we were only able to come upon a correct form of Say's Law by resolving the inconsistency we uncovered in Model A. We thereby came upon Model B which is a correct form of the classical system. Then we found that there is a correct form of the Law in the latter system.

This is because Model B's behavioral character acts, as it were, like a sieve to remove from the system, the invalid elements and role we discussed in Chapter 6.7, that characterize the Say's Law of Model A.

These had entered Model A because the system is an incorrect form of the classical system, a form of the system that has a restricted approach to the behavior of individuals and firms. This, in turn, led to Model A reflecting an incorrect form of the Law that restricts the system to long-run states.

Model B, however, reflects a correct form of the Law in being rid of the inconsistency of Model A; and this correct form of the Law cannot possibly restrict Model B to long-run states or restrict the system in any other way.

17.5 The Rational Behavior Of Model B Resolves The Issue Of Say's Law

Underlying Model A is the maximizing behavior of individuals and firms although we left this behavior implicit in our analysis. However, while Model A is consistent with the maximizing behavior of individuals and firms, and hence with the rational behavior this implies, the system yet lacks a key aspect to behavior.

This is because Model A does not reflect how we must take individuals and firms to be aware that their resources are limited and hence they act in light of this awareness. As a result, Model A, and similar orthodox systems, lack the aspect to rational behavior, discussed in Chapter 6.9, into which this behavior translates.

That is, the orthodox systems do not reflect how individuals and firms, acting rationally, determine their demands and supplies in the knowledge or awareness that their resources are limited.

This assists us in showing how the issue of the Law was resolved which requires that we deal with a variable that is a vehicle for or implies a correct form of Say's Law. This is the variable W which we formed by our collapsing the aggregate demand and supply variables in the Say's Law identity into the single variable W.

Now Model B reflects how individuals and firms, acting rationally, determine their demands and supplies in the knowledge or awareness that their resources are limited. This, in turn, endows the W of Model B with utility since it becomes the system's budget constraint.

Moreover, as would be expected, this brought W into the behavioral content of Model B. Functions $f(z)$ and $g(z)$ then operate on W to determine the quantities of commodities demanded and supplied.

This is how we formed Model B through which we resolved the economic inconsistency of Model A as well as how this inconsistency is reflected in the latter system in mathematical terms. Next, in resolving this inconsistency through Model B, we resolved the issue of Say's Law.

This is because when, with reference to Model B, we dealt with the variable W, we were really dealing implicitly with Say's Law since W is a vehicle for or implies a correct form of the Law. This is because we formed W by collapsing the aggregate demand and supply variables in the Say's Law identity into the single variable W.

Hence W implies a correct form of Say's Law since this variable could only have been formed by our taking the Law as a true identity. Consequently, since W entered the behavioral content of Model B, Say's Law, albeit implicitly, entered the system but in a correct or consistent form.

This is a form of the Law that is rid of the invalid aggregate demand and supply variables of Model A's Say's Law as well as being rid of the invalid use of these variables to make the latter system mathematically consistent.

As a result, a correct form of the Law entered Model B in the sense of being implied by the variable W that enters the system. This is a form of the Law that is solely a descriptive device in the system.

That is, a form of the Law that simply reflects us describing W alternately as aggregate demand and supply. Hence we may re-create the Law in Model B in the form of the identity $ad \equiv as$. That is, by describing W alternately as aggregate demand and supply.

However, this identity clearly has no substantive influence in Model B in being solely a descriptive device in the system. Whereas this identity is given a substantive role in Model A, to account for an incorrect form of the Law characterizing this system.

17.6 Summary

We discussed in the chapter how many controversies about Say's Law focused on whether or not the Law is an identity. However, these controversies had to be resolved on other grounds since the Law in both Model A and Model B is an identity.

This was through our finding that the Law in Model B is a correct form of the Law because it mirrors or is associated with the consistency and generality of the system. Whereas the Law in

Model A is incorrect because it mirrors or is associated with the inconsistency and restricted generality of this system.

We also discussed how the issue of the Law could not be settled on the grounds as to whether or not the Law is part of the classical system. This was through our showing that we first had to arrive at a consistent form of the classical system, Model B; and within this system we found a correct form of the Law.

Finally, we discussed how the issue of Say's Law was resolved through the new approach to rational behavior that characterizes Model B, our revised classical system.

Chapter 18

Limitations Of The Keynesian System

18.1 Introduction

We provided in this book a microeconomic solution to the problem of the classical system being restricted to long-run states. Whereas we shall consider Keynes' solution to this problem as being a macroeconomic solution. However, we shall find that this macroeconomic solution is a restricted one.

This is because it leads to the Keynesian macroeconomic system being an alternative to the classical microeconomic system. Hence the Keynesian and classical systems are dichotomized. Moreover, the Keynesian system does not have a satisfactory basis in microeconomics.

18.2 A Microeconomic Solution To The Restriction Of Model A To Long-Run States

We resolved the inconsistency we uncovered in Model A, through Model B, by generalizing the orthodox microeconomic analysis that is the basis of Model A. This was through our bringing into Model B, the aspect to behavior and the associated aspect to rational behavior we have described, that are missing from Model A.

Moreover, in resolving the inconsistency in Model A's microeconomics through Model B, we also rid the latter system of an incorrect form of Say's Law that restricts Model A to long-run states. Hence Model B is not restricted to long-run states but will move to short-run states were behavior to change to short-run behavior.

This means that systems that emerge when Model B moves to short-run states will, like Model B, also be based on our more general form of microeconomics. Hence we extended our more general approach to microeconomics to macroeconomic or short-run systems.

We arrived in this way at our new approach to price systems, an approach that integrated microeconomic and macroeconomic systems. Let us now consider Keynes' solution to the problem of the restriction of the classical system to long-run states.

18.3 Keynes' Macroeconomic Solution To The Restriction Of Model A To Long-Run States

We may look on Keynes as providing a macroeconomic solution to the problem of Model A being restricted to long-run states. This is an approach which, unlike the approach of this book, is based largely on aggregate demand and supply functions, functions that are not derived from the maximizing behavior of the individual and the firm.

However, we should ideally form macroeconomic price systems by basing them on the maximizing behavior of the individual and the firm and hence on microeconomic analysis; or we should, at least, ensure that the systems are consistent, in principle, with the maximizing behavior of the individual and the firm as is the case with our new systems.

This requires that we find the source of macroeconomics within microeconomic systems along the lines discussed in this book in Chapter 14. However, the classical microeconomic system, when represented by Model A, is necessarily restricted to long-run states. Hence the system's macroeconomic character is suppressed.

Consequently, it seemed that to form a macroeconomic system, we needed a system like the Keynesian system that is an alternative to the classical system. This, however, led to a dichotomy between the microeconomic Model A and the macroeconomic Keynesian system.

However, we resolved this dichotomy by resolving, through Model B, the inconsistency we uncovered in Model A's microeconomics; since in so doing, we rid Model B of Model A's incorrect form of Say's Law that restricts the latter system to long-run states.

Hence Model B is not necessarily restricted to long-run states but will move to short-run states were behavior to change to short-run behavior. Moreover, the short-run systems that emerge from Model B as behavior in the latter system changes to short-run behavior will, like Model B, reflect a consistent microeconomics.

This reflects how through Model B, we resolved the dichotomy between microeconomic and macroeconomic systems.

164

Whereas, as we discussed, Keynes' approach led to his macroeconomic system and the microeconomic Model A being dichotomized. Moreover, unlike our new systems, there is no satisfactory microeconomic basis for Keynes' macroeconomic system.

18.4 Microeconomic And Macroeconomic Solutions To The Restriction Of Model A To Long-Run States

We have discussed how Model A's functions lead to the system being initially inconsistent in a mathematical sense. Then the system is made consistent by Say's Law being imposed on it to eliminate a surplus equation to make the system mathematically consistent.

This form of the Law is reflected in the identity $ad{\equiv}as$ which, as we discussed in Chapter 6.7, is created from the variable W in order to eliminate Model A's surplus equation.

Next, since this identity, in putting aggregate demand identical to aggregate supply, caused Model A to be restricted to long-run states, it also seemed that the solution to this was to allow aggregate demand and supply to diverge. Then aggregate demand and supply, in coming to equilibrium, would determine overall output or income.

This, of course, is the approach Keynes adopted which led to his short-run system, an approach that is macroeconomic in character. However, this led to the microeconomics of the real part of the Keynesian system being suppressed. In contrast, our approach to the Law is quite different from Keynes' approach.

We showed in Chapter 6.4 that Model B, our revised form of Model A, is automatically consistent in a mathematical sense. Hence we do not need Say's Law to make Model B mathematically consistent; and this rid Model B of Model A's incorrect form of the Law.

As a result, we rid Model B of Model A's incorrect form of the Law through microeconomic analysis; since it is Model B's microeconomic functions that ensure that the system is automatically consistent in a mathematical sense.

Next, Model A's incorrect form of Say's Law had brought long-run market processes into the latter system. Hence as would be expected, Model B's demand and supply functions brought long-run market processes into Model B as was confirmed in Chapter 6.5.

Moreover, this meant that since these functions brought one form of behavior, long-run behavior, into the system, they may be made to reflect other forms of behavior such as short-run behavior. Consequently, Model B will move from a long-run state to short-run states were behavior to change to short-run behavior, the system hence having a macroeconomic character.

Yet Model B, and hence systems that emerge from it as it moves to alternative states, are all microeconomic systems in being based wholly on microeconomic behavior. That is, on the behavior of the individual and the firm.

18.5 How The Alternative Solutions To The Restriction Of Model A To Long-Run States Arose

We have discussed how Model A, the orthodox classical system, is initially inconsistent in a mathematical sense. Then Say's Law is imposed on the system to make it mathematically consistent. Moreover, we showed that the Law implies the variable W which reflects the system's long-run output or income.

Hence W is imposed on Model A in a non-behavioral manner which restricts the system to long-run states. Keynes then proceeded to make the overall output of his system behaviorally determined to give his system a macroeconomic character .

Keynes, however, took overall output W as meaning overall output that is of relevance only to macroeconomic systems, and gave it a behavioral character. Next, W is determined by Keynes' aggregate demand and supply functions; but these functions suppress or abstract from the microeconomics of the real part of the Keynesian system.

However, what is required is that W be taken to reflect both of the meanings that we have discussed earlier in the book. That is, as both overall output of relevance to macroeconomic systems and as a budget constraint of relevance to microeconomic systems; and this is the case with Model B.

That is, the overall output or income variable W of Model B is of relevance to macroeconomic systems which gives the system a macroeconomic character. However, this overall output variable W of Model B is also consistent with the latter system being a microeconomic system.

This is because this overall output or income variable also reflects Model B's budget or income constraint; and this budget constraint provides the basis for the maximizing behavior of the individual and the firm. Hence Model B, while having a macroeconomic character, is a microeconomic system in being based wholly on the behavior of the individual and the firm.

Consequently, both Model B and the Keynesian system have a macroeconomic character in that both systems can move to alternative states as behavior changes. However, the microeconomics of the real part of the Keynesian system is suppressed. Whereas Model B is wholly microeconomic in character.

18.6 The Rationale Of The New Price Systems

Clearly, the approach to price systems set out in the book traces to the new aspect to behavior, and associated rational behavior, underlying our new systems. This accounted for our new systems having a more general character compared to both orthodox microeconomic and macroeconomic systems.

Let us illustrate this by first comparing Model B, which represents our new systems, to Model A, the orthodox classical system. Then we shall compare Model B with the Keynesian system.

As was discussed in Chapter 2.3, we brought an aspect to behavior that is missing from Model A into Model B. This aspect to behavior is reflected in individuals and firms being taken to be aware that their resources are limited and hence they act in light of this awareness.

This behavior, in turn, as was discussed in Chapter 6.9, translated into the rational behavior underlying Model B's demand and supply functions. This is that individuals and firms, acting rationally, determine their demands and supplies in the knowledge or awareness that their resources are limited.

This gave utility to individuals and firms of a variable that we denoted by W, that reflects their limited resources or budget constraint.

This variable reflects the overall output or income of Model B as well as the system's limited resources or budget constraint; although, as we pointed out in Chapter 5.10, the limited resources of individuals and firms would have to be more broadly defined in more detailed and complex forms of Model B.

Next, the variable W entered Model B as a budget constraint resulting in it entering the system's demand and supply functions; and this provided the means whereby individuals and firms are made aware that their resources are limited.

Moreover, individuals and firms act in light of this awareness. This is through the interior functions $f(z)$ and $g(z)$ that are internal to Model B's overall demand and supply functions, operating on W to determine individual quantities of commodities demanded and supplied.

This reflected how Model B is based on microeconomic behavior. Yet the system also has a macroeconomic character; and this also stems from the rational behavior underlying the system.

As we have discussed, the variable W of Model B enters the system's demand and supply functions. This, in turn, as was discussed in Chapter 6.7, led to the Say's Law of Model B being rid of invalid elements and an invalid role that characterize the Law in Model A.

These had led to Model A reflecting an incorrect form of the Law, a form of the Law that restricts the system to long-run states. However, since the Law in Model B was rid of the invalid elements and role that characterize Model A's form of the Law, a correct form of Say's Law entered Model B.

This is a form of the Law which, as was confirmed in Chapter 9, cannot possibly restrict Model B to long-run states. As a result, Model B will move to short-run states were behavior to change. Hence the system has a macroeconomic character. Whereas the macroeconomic character of Model A is suppressed.

Let us now compare Model B with the Keynesian macroeconomic system. Both systems have a macroeconomic character. Hence the systems are both characterized by a behaviorally-determined overall output or income variable that we denoted by W.

However, the W of the Keynesian system abstracts from or suppresses the microeconomic market processes of the real part of the Keynesian system.

This is because this W directly enters the markets of the Keynesian system where it is determined by aggregate demand and supply functions through an aggregative market equilibrating process. As a result, the microeconomics of the real part of the Keynesian system is suppressed. Let us now consider Model B.

Model B is similar to the Keynesian system in that like the latter system, Model B is also characterized by a behaviorally-determined overall output or income variable W. This reflects how both systems have a macroeconomic character. Yet Model B differs in a basic way from the Keynesian system.

This is because the overall output variable W of Model B does not directly enter the markets of Model B. Were this the case, the microeconomic market processes of Model B would be suppressed just as the microeconomic market processes of the real part of the Keynesian system are suppressed.

Instead, on account of the rational behavior of Model B, the overall output or income variable W of Model B also reflects the limited resources or budget constraint of the system; and W enters Model B as a budget constraint to also enter the system's demand and supply functions.

Next, functions $f(z)$ and $g(z)$ that are also within Model B's demand and supply functions, operate on W to determine individual quantities of commodities demanded and supplied. These then enter the markets of Model B. Hence Model B is a wholly microeconomic system yet the system also has a macroeconomic character.

Consequently, Model B has a more general character compared to both the orthodox classical microeconomic system, Model A, and the Keynesian macroeconomic system. This explains why Model B provided the basis to integrate microeconomic and macroeconomic systems.

18.7 Notes On The Classical And Neoclassical Systems

This book has brought up issues concerning how Keynes interpreted the classical system and how the system was interpreted in this book.

We discussed in Chapter 13 how we may look on Model B as a classical system since it was derived or elicited from basic elements associated with the classical system. However, we pointed out that key behavioral aspects of Model B are not brought out in the classical literature proper and the later literature on the classical and neoclassical systems.

On the other hand, we must take Model A as a neoclassical system, a system we corrected through Model B in that through the latter system, we resolved the inconsistency we uncovered in Model A. Yet we initially took Model A as reflecting the classical system.

However, while we have now seen that Model A is not a correct classical system, we initially took it as a classical system to assist us in understanding Keynesian analysis. We came to this conclusion primarily because Model A reflects Keynes' basic criticism of the classical system which is that the system is restricted to long-run states by Say's Law.

Hence in taking Model A initially to reflect the classical system, we focused on a system that confirms Keynes' view of the system. This, in turn, allowed us to better understand the Keynesian system along the lines we have discussed, and to bring out basic problems with the system.

18.8 Summary

We resolved the problem of the orthodox classical system being restricted to long-run states through a microeconomic approach to the system. This is an approach whereby in resolving the hidden inconsistency of Model A, through Model B, we rid the latter system of a restricted approach to microeconomic analysis that characterizes Model A. Hence Model B reflects a more general approach to microeconomics compared to Model A.

Moreover, in bringing a more general approach to microeconomics into Model B, we also rid the system of an incorrect form of Say's Law of Model A that restricts the latter system to long-run states. This means that Model B is not restricted to long-run states hence the system will move to short-run states were behavior to change to short-run behavior.

As a result, the short-run systems that emerge from Model B will, like Model B, also be characterized by a consistent microeconomics. This reflected our microeconomic solution to the problem of Model A being restricted to long-run states.

On the other hand, we could describe Keynes' approach to resolving the problem of the classical system being restricted to long-run states as a macroeconomic approach. However, this latter approach led to Keynes' macroeconomic system being an alternative to the classical microeconomic system. Moreover, the microeconomics of the real part of the Keynesian system is suppressed.

Chapter 19

Summarizing The Book

19.1 Introduction

We have uncovered in this book, an inconsistency in the general economic logic or rationale of orthodox price systems. This inconsistency arose because the systems lack a consistent general economic logic or rationale that extends across all of the systems.

Hence the systems lack an aspect to the behavior of individuals and firms that should ensure that the systems reflect this economic logic; and this restricts the generality of the systems.

However, we brought this aspect to the behavior of individuals and firms, and an associated aspect to rational behavior, into our new systems, to resolve the inconsistency in the orthodox systems. This led to a more general approach to price systems compared to the orthodox approach.

There are many consequences of this new approach to price systems. However, we focused on how this new approach integrates systems that are based on this approach.

This is in the sense that the systems based on our new approach, irrespective of the different forms of behavior of individual systems, are united or integrated by the general economic logic that stems from our new approach to price systems.

Consequently, our new approach to price systems integrated orthodox microeconomic and macroeconomic systems, systems which are dichotomized; and this integration was hence also be in terms of the systems' general economic logic or rationale.

We proceeded by focusing on a specific system that represents our new systems, in order to show precisely how we integrate microeconomic and macroeconomic systems. This is a revised classical system which was be formed by our ridding the orthodox classical system of the inconsistency we uncovered in orthodox price systems.

This revised classical system reflects a more general approach to microeconomics compared to the orthodox approach.

This is because this revised classical system reflects the aspect to behavior, and associated rational behavior, that are missing from the orthodox systems.

Next, we showed that our revised classical system, while being a long-run system, is not necessarily restricted to long-run states like the orthodox classical system. Hence the revised classical system can move to short-run states were behavior to change to short-run behavior.

That is, short-run or macroeconomic systems emerge from our revised classical system as behavior in the system changes to short-run behavior. Moreover, these short-run or macroeconomic systems reflect the similar general logic that characterizes our revised classical system itself.

This reflected how we integrated microeconomic and macroeconomic systems from the perspective of microeconomic systems as represented by our revised classical system. Moreover, we drew on our new approach to price systems in Chapter 16.4, to show how the Keynesian macroeconomic system may, in principle, be given a satisfactory microeconomic character.

Hence our new approach to price systems provided a means to integrate microeconomic and macroeconomic systems from the perspective of both microeconomic and macroeconomic systems.

Consequently, our new approach to price systems, as reflected in our revised classical system, is more general than the orthodox approach. This is because this new approach ensures that all systems based on this approach are integrated.

This, to review, is in the sense that this approach brings into price systems, a common and consistent general economic logic. This unites the systems in terms of this general economic logic while allowing for the different forms of behavior of individual systems.

Whereas the orthodox approach to price systems does not bring such a common and consistent general economic logic into orthodox systems. This is because of the inconsistency we have uncovered that characterizes the orthodox approach to price systems.

This explains why orthodox price systems, such as microeconomic and macroeconomic systems, are dichotomized; since they lack the unifying general economic logic that characterizes our new systems.

This has been a very general description of the inconsistency we have uncovered in orthodox price systems; and we had to put the general economic logic of price systems in a way that allowed us to put our analysis into mathematical terms. This was be done in the following way.

All price systems are subject to limitation in resources hence the systems must reflect consistency with limitation in resources. That is, the quantities of goods demanded and the quantities supplied must each sum to a limited volume of resources underlying the systems.

Consequently, since all price systems must necessarily be consistent with limitation in resources, we could look on consistency with limitation in resources as reflecting the general economic logic that should extend across all price systems.

Next, we discussed how we shall bring into our new systems, an aspect to behavior that will bring the general logic of price systems into our new systems; and this aspect to behavior captured consistency with limitation in resources in a manner that takes such consistency as a property of all of our new systems or of price systems in general.

This accounted for the generality of our new approach to price systems. However, orthodox price systems lack the aspect to behavior we have described that characterizes our new systems; and this results in the orthodox systems being initially inconsistent in a mathematical sense.

Then the systems are made mathematically consistent; and this ensures that the systems are consistent with limitation in resources. However, while mathematical consistency ensures consistency of the orthodox systems with limitation in resources, this is ensured in a restricted manner.

This is because mathematical consistency ensures consistency of orthodox price systems with limitation in resources only as a property of each individual system rather than as a property that extends over all the systems.

Hence while each individual orthodox system is consistent with limitation in resources, the systems yet lack the general economic logic or rationale that extends across all price systems.

This is because this requires that consistency with limitation in resources be ensured in a manner that takes such consistency as a property of price systems in general. This, however, is not the case with orthodox systems; and this restricts the generality of the systems.

19.2 Generalizing The Orthodox Classical System

Clearly, the key to the book lies in our generalizing the orthodox classical system, Model A, through ridding it of the inconsistency we have uncovered in the system. Model A is initially inconsistent in a mathematical sense. Then the system is made consistent by being made mathematically consistent.

As a result, consistency of a system should be ensured by the economic rationale of the system rather than by the system being made mathematically consistent. Next, Model A is made mathematically consistent by Say's Law being used to eliminate a surplus equation from the system.

However, in Chapter 5.4, we collapsed the aggregate demand and supply variables in the Say's Law identity into the single variable W. This variable reflects the overall output or income of Model A; but we showed that it also reflects the limited resources or budget constraint of the system.

This collapsing of Say's Law into the single variable W meant that the Law could not now be used to ensure mathematical consistency of Model A. This, however, is where the new aspect to behavior, and associated rational behavior of Model B, came into the picture.

This new aspect to behavior, as was discussed in Chapter 6.9, is reflected in our taking individuals and firms to be aware that their resources are limited and hence they act in light of this awareness. Moreover, this translated into a new approach to rational behavior. This is that individuals and firms, acting rationally, determine their demands and supplies in the knowledge that their resources are limited.

Then in Chapter 6.6, we incorporated this behavior into the new type of demand and supply functions that characterize Model B, our revised form of Model A; and we found that unlike Model A, Model B is automatically consistent in a mathematical sense. Hence we did not need the Law to make Model B mathematically consistent which brought a correct form of the Law into the latter system.

Consequently, our new approach to behavior rid Model B of Model A's incorrect form of Say's Law. This was then replaced by a correct identity form of the Law in Model B as was confirmed in Chapter 9.

Now the Say's Law that was imposed on Model A to make the system consistent restricts the system to long-run states. This suppresses the system's macroeconomic character; since for a system to have a macroeconomic it must be able to move to alternative states as behavior changes.

As a result, Model B, in being rid of Model A's form of Say's Law, is not restricted to long-run states. Hence Model B can move to alternative states as behavior changes, a reflection of the system having a macroeconomic character.

However, Model B was thereby given a macroeconomic character only in principle. This is because the system required an actual means through which it may be moved to alternative states as behavior changes.

This is brought into Model B, as in all macroeconomic systems, by a behaviorally-determined overall output or income variable that we denoted by W. Hence as behavior changes, to change W, Model B will move to alternative states such as short-run states. As a result, Model B has a macroeconomic character like the Keynesian system.

Yet Model B is more general than the Keynesian system in that Model B is a wholly microeconomic system. Whereas the microeconomics of the real part of the Keynesian system is suppressed. We were able to bring out this difference between the systems by drawing on the condition for internal consistency of a macroeconomic system that was set out in Chapter 5.3.

This is that the way in which a system is rid of Model A's form of Say's Law, to give the system, in principle, a macroeconomic character, must be consistent with the nature of the system's overall output or income variable; and both Model B and the Keynesian system meet this condition.

However, this condition is met in the Keynesian system through macroeconomic analysis; and this accounts for the microeconomics of the real part of the Keynesian system being suppressed. Let us now review how Model B met the condition for internal consistency of a macroeconomic system; since it was in establishing this that we fully brought out why Model B is more general than the Keynesian system.

Keynes removed Model A's Say's Law from his system through macroeconomic analysis; and this resulted in his overall output variable W also being macroeconomic in character. However, we removed Model A's Say's Law from Model B through microeconomic analysis. This was through our resolving the inconsistency we uncovered within Model A through Model B.

Hence it was through microeconomic analysis that Model B, in principle, is made able to move among alternative states. Next, Model B, like the Keynesian system, also required a behaviorally-determined overall output or income variable W.

However, this W in Model B now had to be consistent with the microeconomic approach whereby we rid Model B of Model A's Say's Law. That is, the W in Model B had to be consistent with the system's microeconomics.

This was ensured through W entering the behavioral content of Model B as a budget constraint. Then Model B's internal functions that rid the system of Model A's Say's Law, operate on the W in Model B to determine individual quantities of commodities demanded and supplied.

This reflects how the overall output or income variable W of Model B's is consistent with the system's microeconomic character. Hence it is consistent with how the system, in the first place, was made consistent, in principle, with having a macroeconomic character through microeconomic analysis.

This meant that Model B has a macroeconomic character yet the system is a microeconomic system in being based wholly on the behavior of the individual and the firm. This is a very general approach to establishing that Model B. which is a microeconomic system, yet has a macroeconomic character.

However, we also established this through showing how our general condition for internal consistency of macroeconomic systems stems from Model B's microeconomic demand and supply functions.

We discussed in Chapter 6.7 how the variable W, that reflects Model B's overall output or income, is brought into the behavioral content of the system by the system's internal functions. These are functions that bring our new aspect to behavior that we have we described into Model B. This, in turn, transforms W to also reflect the system's limited resources or budget constraint.

Moreover, the movement of W into the behavioral content of Model B, as was also discussed in Chapter 6.7, rids the system of Model A's incorrect form of Say's Law that restricts the latter system to long-run states. Hence Model B is not restricted in this way.

Consequently, Model B will move to alternative states as behavior changes, the system hence having a macroeconomic character. This illustrates how Model B's microeconomic functions are consistent with our general condition for internal consistency of macroeconomic systems.

Hence the macroeconomic character of Model B arose out of the system's microeconomics; since we were only able to elicit the system's macroeconomic character through correctly capturing the behavior of the individual and the firm in this system through Model B's demand and supply functions. Whereas Model A's macroeconomic character is suppressed because the behavior of the individual and the firm is not captured correctly in this system.

To review, Model A is initially inconsistent in a mathematical sense. Say's Law is then imposed on the system to make it mathematically consistent; and this imposes on Model A, the variable W that reflects the system's overall or income.

However, this variable remains outside the behavioral content of Model A hence it cannot be brought into the system's behavioral content as a budget constraint as in Model B. As a result, Model A remains characterized by an incorrect form of Say's Law that restricts the system to long-run states.

Clearly, these problems arose because Model A's functions, in not correctly reflecting the behavior of the individual and the firm, are inconsistent with our general condition for internal consistency of macroeconomic systems. This explains why Model A's macroeconomic character is suppressed.

19.3 Review Of The Hidden Inconsistency In The Orthodox Classical System

We first discussed the inconsistency we uncovered in the orthodox classical system in a general way in Chapter 1. To review, there are two basic facets to price systems: First, there is a general logic to the systems that extends across all of the systems. This is reflected in all systems being consistent with limitation in resources. Second, there is the behavior that characterizes individual systems.

However, Model A, the orthodox form of the classical system, while reflecting the classical approach to long-run behavior, does not correctly reflect the general logic of economic behavior that should characterize all price systems.

This is because the system does not reflect how behavior in all price systems, irrespective of the different forms of behavior of individual systems, must be behavior that is consistent with limitation in resources. This results in Model A capturing consistency with limitation in resources as a property of this specific system rather than as a property of price systems in general.

This brings inconsistency into Model A which accounts for the system being restricted to long-run states and also mars the system in other ways. We also discussed this inconsistency in more detail in Chapter 2.

Model A is inconsistent in an economic sense because the system lacks an aspect to the behavior of individuals and firms. This is the aspect to behavior that ensures that a system is consistent with limitation in resources.

More precisely, it is the aspect to behavior reflected in individuals and firms having to be taken to be aware that their resources are limited and hence they act in light of this awareness. As a result, since this aspect to behavior is missing from Model A, the system's functions do not ensure that the system is consistent with limitation in resources.

This, in turn, causes the system to be initially inconsistent in a mathematical sense. Economists then proceed to make the system consistent by making it mathematically consistent; and this ensures that the system is consistent with limitation in resources.

However, Model A remains inconsistent in an economic sense; since the system's economic inconsistency can only be satisfactorily resolved by revising the system's functions to make them ensure that the system is consistent with limitation in resources.

This is the course followed in the book through Model B; since Model B's functions ensure that the latter system is consistent with limitation in resources. That is, Model B's functions ensure that the quantities of commodities demanded and supplied each sum to the limited volume of resources underlying the system.

Hence through Model B, we resolved Model A's economic inconsistency. Moreover, Model B is automatically consistent in a mathematical sense. As a result, through Model B, we resolved Model A's economic inconsistency as well as how this inconsistency is reflected in Model A in mathematical terms.

We shall now review how we arrived at our new type of demand and supply functions of Model B through which we resolved the inconsistency of Model A.

19.4 Finding The New Type Of Demand And Supply Functions

Model A's economic inconsistency results in mathematical consistency being given precedence over economic consistency in ensuring that the system is consistent with limitation in resources.

However, we found, as was discussed in Chapter 5, that mathematical consistency ensures that the system is consistent with limitation in resources by transforming quantities into relative quantities. This transformation of quantities into relative quantities then ensures that these quantities always sum to the limited volume of resources of the system.

This is because in being relative quantities, these quantities will adjust in a relative manner to always sum to the limited volume of resources of the system. This provided a clue as to the form of our new type of demand and supply functions through which we resolved Model A's hidden inconsistency.

To review, mathematical consistency of Model A ensures consistency of the system with limited resources through transforming quantities into relative quantities.

This raised the possibility that there may be another way, other than through making the system mathematically consistent, to transform quantities into relative quantities to make the system consistent with limitation in resources.

This, as we showed, was to write demand and supply functions that themselves determine relative quantities of commodities demanded and relative quantities supplied. This led to our new type of functions, our relative demand and supply functions, that were set out in detail in Chapter 6.

These formed the basis for Model B, our revised form of Model A. Then through Model B, we resolved the hidden economic inconsistency of Model A as well as how this inconsistency is reflected in Model A in mathematical terms, analyses we summarized in Chapter 8.

19.5 Generalizing The Orthodox Microeconomic Analysis

Individuals and firms in orthodox microeconomic systems are conceived of as demanding and supplying goods to maximize their utility and profit subject to a budget constraint; and our new systems are consistent with this behavior but generalizes it.

This is through our bringing into the orthodox microeconomic analysis, an aspect to the behavior of the individual and the firm that is missing from this analysis. To review, functions $f(z)$ and $g(z)$ of Model B that are within the system's overall demand and supply functions, operate on the

179

variable W to determine the quantities of commodities demanded and supplied.

Next, the variable W reflects the overall output of the system; but as discussed in Chapter 5, it also simultaneously reflects the limited resources or budget constraint of individuals and firms.

Hence taking it that individuals and firms in Model B maximize their utility and profit subject to a budget constraint, we must assume that the quantities determined in Model B by functions $f(z)$ and the $g(z)$ operating on W, are a consequence of this maximizing behavior.

Moreover, not only is Model B, albeit implicitly, consistent with the maximizing behavior of individuals and firms along the lines discussed. Model B's functions also reflect an aspect to the behavior of individuals and firms that is missing from the orthodox microeconomic analysis.

This is the aspect to behavior reflected in us taking individuals and firms to be aware that their resources are limited and hence they act in light of this awareness; and this behavior translated, as we discussed in Chapter 6.9, into an aspect to rational behavior that is hence also missing from the orthodox microeconomic analysis.

As a result, we generalized the orthodox microeconomic analysis by incorporating into it, an aspect to the behavior of individuals and firms, and an associated aspect to rational behavior, that are is missing from the orthodox analysis.

This accounted for our new functions that characterize Model B, resolving the hidden inconsistency of Model A; and as well, it explains why our new systems, while being microeconomic systems, yet have a macroeconomic character.

This is because Model B's functions not only bring a more general approach to microeconomics into the system. The functions, as well, rid Model B of an incorrect form of Say's Law that characterizes Model A and which restricts the latter system to long-run states.

Hence Model B is not restricted to long-run states which means that the system will move to short-run states were behavior to change to short-run behavior. This means that Model B has a macroeconomic character; and this is due to the more general form of microeconomics on which we have based the system, an approach to microeconomics we arrived at through resolving the hidden inconsistency of Model A.

19.6 Model B's Macroeconomic Character Stems From The System's Microeconomics

We have discussed how on account of Model B's microeconomics, we rid the system of an incorrect form of Say's Law that restricts Model A to long-run states. Hence Model B is not restricted in this way, which means that the system will move to alternative states as behavior changes. This gives Model B a macroeconomic character but only in principle; and this brings up another key facet to macroeconomic systems.

This is reflected in macroeconomic systems having a behaviorally-determined overall output or income variable. Hence as behavior changes, this will change overall output or income to actually cause the system to move to alternative states.

However, the Keynesian system's overall output or income variable W is macroeconomic in character. This is reflected in it being determined by aggregate demand and supply functions; but these functions suppress the microeconomics of the real part of the Keynesian system.

This reflects how the Keynesian W is macroeconomic in character, which is consistent with the overall macroeconomic character of the system.

Model B also has to have a behaviorally-determined overall output or income variable. However, this variable in Model B must be consistent with microeconomics since Model B is microeconomic in character; and Model B's overall output variable W is consistent with the system's microeconomics.

This, to review, is because Model B's overall output variable W does not directly enter the market processes of the system as is the case with the W of the Keynesian. Instead, Model B's overall output variable W enters the system as a budget or income constraint.

Model B's interior functions then operate on W to determine individual quantities of commodities demanded and supplied reflecting how the system is microeconomic in character. Hence Model B is characterized by a behaviorally-determined overall output variable W that reflects how the system has a macroeconomic character.

Yet the system is a microeconomic system. This is reflected in the system's overall output variable W being consistent, in the manner discussed, with the system's microeconomic character. This analysis brings out how there is a parallel between the Keynesian system and Model B with regard to how the systems are given a macroeconomic character. Yet Model B is more general than the Keynesian system.

As we discussed in Chapter 5.3, to form a macroeconomic system, we must form a system that, in the first place, is consistent, in principle, with being able to move among alternative states as behavior changes. This is accomplished through the system being rid of Model A's incorrect form of Say's Law.

Moreover, the system must also be characterized by a behaviorally-determined overall output or income variable; and both the Keynesian system and Model B reflect these properties. These properties are also consistent with each other in both Model B and the Keynesian system reflecting how both systems are internally consistent macroeconomic systems.

However, these properties that we have described are brought into the Keynesian system through macroeconomic analysis; and this suppresses the microeconomics of the real part of the Keynesian system.

Whereas these properties are brought into Model B through microeconomic analysis; and this accounts for Model B being a wholly microeconomic system. Yet Model B also has a macroeconomic character in that it can move among alterative states as behavior changes; and this is due to the operation of the system's microeconomic market processes as was discussed in Chapter 7.2.

Consequently, Model B's macroeconomic character, reflected in it being able to move to alternative states, arises out of the system's microeconomics. This reflects how through Model B, we integrate microeconomic and macroeconomic systems.

19.7 Consistency Of The General Logic Of The New Price Systems

This book casts consistency of the general logic of price systems into economic rather than mathematical terms. Economists ensure that the general logic of orthodox price systems is consistent by making the systems mathematically consistent; and mathematical consistency means that we may solve the systems for their equilibrium quantities of commodities and equilibrium prices.

However, we must assume that the systems are subject to limitation in resources. Hence the quantities we solve for as a consequence of making the systems mathematically consistent must sum to the limited volume of resources of the systems.

As a result, consistency with limitation in resources, or consistency of the systems' general economic logic, is ensured in orthodox price systems as a consequence of the systems being made mathematically consistent. This is a reflection of an economic inconsistency in the systems.

This is because it reflects how the systems' demand and supply functions, in the first place, do not ensure that the systems are consistent with limitation in resources. Then the systems are made consistent with limitation in resources as a consequence of being made mathematically consistent.

Hence there is an aspect to behavior missing from the orthodox systems, this being the aspect to behavior that should ensure that the systems are consistent with limitation in resources.

However, we formed a new type of demand and supply functions, our relative demand and supply functions, which ensure consistency of price systems with limited resources; and we based our new systems, as represented by Model B, on these new functions.

This meant that consistency of the general economic logic of our new systems, in reflecting consistency of the systems with limited resources, is ensured by the systems' behavior or economic rationale in being ensured by the systems' demand and supply functions.

Whereas consistency of the general economic logic of orthodox price systems such as Model A, meaning also consistency of the systems with limited resources, is ensured as a consequence of the systems being made mathematically consistent. We could now see why our new approach to price systems is more general than the orthodox approach.

Consistency of the general economic logic of our new systems, meaning consistency of the systems with limited resources, is ensured by the behavior or economic rationale of the systems. This is because it is ensured by the systems' demand and supply functions. Hence any system based on our new type of functions is automatically consistent with limitation in resources.

Orthodox systems, however, are not based on our new type of functions. Yet the systems must also, of course, be consistent with limitation in resources. This, however, is ensured by each of the systems being made mathematically consistent by external budget constraints being imposed on the systems.

This causes our economic condition for consistency with limited resources that applies to all of our new systems, to lose its generality in orthodox systems. This is because this condition is transformed from being an economic condition that applies to all of our new systems, into mathematical conditions that apply to each individual orthodox system.

This, in turn, explains why each individual orthodox system has to be made mathematically consistent by external budget constraints being imposed on them; and this does ensure that each orthodox system is consistent with limitation in resources.

However, this is not ensured by an economic condition such as characterizes our new systems, that applies to price systems in general. Instead, consistency with limited resources is ensured in orthodox price systems as a property of each individual system, rather than as a property of price systems in general; and this restricts the generality of the orthodox systems.

19.8 Resolving The Issue Of Say's Law

Say's Law is an identity or truism hence we should not attribute any substantive role to the Law. However, a substantive role is attributed to the Law in Model A since the Law is used to make the system mathematically consistent; and this brings an incorrect form of the Law into Model A that restricts the system to long-run states.

In contrast, Model B's functions lead to the system being automatically consistent in a mathematical sense. Hence we did not need the Say's Law identity to make Model B consistent; and this rid Model B of an incorrect form of Say's Law that restricts Model A to long-run states.

Consequently, as we discussed in Chapters 6.7 and 6.8, Model B is characterized by a correct form of Say's Law whereas Model A reflects an incorrect for of the Law.

Moreover, as we discussed in Chapter 6.10, Model B's correct Say's Law stems from the new approach to rational behavior underlying the system. Whereas Model A is characterized by an incorrect form of the Law because it lacks this aspect to rational behavior.

To review, we derived the variable W by collapsing the aggregate demand and supply variables in the Say's Law identity of Model A into the single variable W. This variable reflects Model A's overall output or income although we had to elicit it from the system in the manner described.

Next, Model A is initially inconsistent in a mathematical sense. Then Say's Law is imposed on the system to eliminate a surplus equation to make it mathematically consistent. This meant that the variable W, in being implied by the Law, is also imposed on Model A from the outside.

Hence W is outside the system's behavioral content; and this is because Model A lacks the rational behavior that characterizes Model B. This rational behavior, to review, reflects how individuals and firms, acting rationally, determine their demands and supplies in the knowledge or awareness that their resources are limited.

This gives utility to individuals and firms of a variable that reflects their limited resources or budget constraint; and this variable is W. This causes W to move from outside the behavioral content of Model A into the behavioral content of Model B.

This results in the W in Model B also taking on the meaning of a budget constraint that provides the basis for the maximization behavior of individuals and firms.

This is reflected in Model B's interior functions, functions $f(z)$ and $g(z)$, operating respectively on W to determine the quantities of commodities demanded and supplied. We may now readily see how the approach to rational behavior of Model B accounted for us resolving the issue of Say's Law.

We discussed in Chapter 6.7 how the variable W in Model B is the means whereby individuals and firms are made aware that their resources are limited; and this variable was brought into the behavioral content of Model B on account of the rational behavior of individuals and firms.

However, the variable W is implicit in Model A's Say's Law. Hence it had to be removed from this latter system's Say's Law to make it explicit in order for it to enter the behavioral content of Model B. This was accomplished by our collapsing the aggregate demand and supply variables in the Say's Law identity into the single variable W.

Consequently, it is the rational behavior of Model B that required that W be removed from the Say's Law of Model A in order that it may enter the behavioral content of Model B.

Moreover, once we collapsed the Law to form the variable W, the Law could not now be used to ensure mathematical consistency of Model A. However, this is where the new approach to behavior in Model B came into the picture.

As we discussed in Chapter 6.4, Model B is automatically consistent in a mathematical sense. Hence we did not need Say's

Law to make the system mathematically consistent; and this rid Model B of Model A's incorrect form of the Law.

As a result, since it is the behavior underlying Model B that accounts for the system being automatically consistent in a mathematical sense, it is this behavior that resolved the issue of Say's Law. Hence by the same token, it is because Model A lacks the behavior that characterizes Model B, that Model A reflects an incorrect form of the Law.

We also discussed from an alternative perspective in Chapter 17.5, how the rational behavior of Model B accounts for us resolving the issue of Say's Law. This analysis centered on the variable W which, to review, was derived by our collapsing the aggregate demand and supply variables in the Say's Law identity to form the single variable W.

This meant that W reflects or is a vehicle for a true form of the Law in that it could only have been derived by our taking the Law as a true identity. Next, we have discussed how W entered the behavioral content of Model B. This meant that Model B reflects a correct form of the Law.

This is in the sense that we may re-create the Law within the system by describing W alternately as aggregate demand and supply. Clearly, however, this is a correct form of the Law in that it is solely a descriptive device in the system.

We also discussed other issues concerning Say's Law in Chapter 17. Most generally, we showed there that the Law in Model B is a correct form of the Law because it mirrors or is associated with the consistency and generality of the system. Whereas the Law in Model A is incorrect because it mirrors or is associated with the inconsistency and restricted generality of the system.

19.9 A Unified Approach To Price Systems

This book has provided a unified approach to price systems by going beyond the specific forms of behavior of individual systems, to uncover the general economic logic or rationale that characterizes all price systems.

That is, we showed that price systems, while having different forms of behavior, are all united by a common and consistent general economic logic; and this integrates the systems. This was mirrored in the new type of demand and supply functions on which we based our new systems. These are our relative demand and supply functions.

These functions, although developed in detail in the book for our revised classical long-run system may, in principle, be made to reflect the various forms of behavior of other systems. Nonetheless, the relative character of the functions will ensure that all systems based on this type of functions reflect the common and consistent general economic logic, and associated behavior, that underlies our new systems.

This was accomplished by our imposing on our new systems, through the relative character of the systems' demand and supply functions, a condition for general economic consistency of the systems. This is that consistency of the systems with limitation in resources be ensured by the behavior or economic rationale of the systems. This is a condition that applies across all price systems.

Next, we had to find the behavior that underlies this economic condition; and clearly, this behavior also had to be relevant to all of our new systems or to price systems in general. This was the case, since this behavior is reflected in our taking individuals and firms to be aware that their resources are limited and hence they act in light of this awareness.

This behavior, and the rational behavior we described into which it translates, are clearly relevant to all price systems or to price systems in general. We then integrated this behavior into Model B, our revised classical system, through the system's demand and supply functions.

Hence Model B reflects the general economic logic or rationale that should characterize all price systems. This explained why through our new approach to price systems, as reflected in Model B, we integrated microeconomic and macroeconomic price systems.

Whereas orthodox microeconomic and macroeconomic systems are dichotomized because they lack this common and consistent general economic logic. We may best bring out the generality of our new approach to price systems by comparing Model B, our revised classical system, with Model A, the orthodox form of the classical system.

Model B has a more general character than Model A in that Model B, unlike Model A, reflects the general economic logic that is relevant to all price systems. Moreover, this accounts for Model B being automatically consistent in a mathematical sense.

However, Model A is not characterized by Model B's general economic logic; and this results in the system being initially inconsistent in a mathematical sense. Economists then make Model A mathematically consistent by imposing Say's Law on the system to eliminate a surplus equation; and this ensures consistency of the system with limitation in resources.

This, however, brings the inconsistency we have uncovered into the system; since consistency of Model A with limitation in resources should be ensured, as in Model B, by the behavior or economic rationale of the system rather than by the system being made mathematically consistent.

Moreover, mathematical consistency of Model A ensures consistency of the system with limitation in resources only as a property of the specific Model A. Hence Model A, unlike Model B, loses consistency with limitation in resources as a general economic property that applies across all price systems. This accounts for the restricted generality of Model A compared to Model B.

We also illustrated our unified approach to price systems through how we dealt with a key variable that should characterize all price systems.

This is the overall output or income variable that is associated with macroeconomic systems such as the Keynesian system. This variable should be a means of integrating price systems; but it accounts for orthodox systems being dichotomized.

This is reflected in Keynes taking this variable in the restricted sense of reflecting only the overall output or income of macroeconomic systems; and this results in the microeconomics of the real part of the Keynesian system being suppressed.

However, we gave the overall output or income variable a broader meaning in Model B; since in this latter system, this variable reflects not only the overall output or income of the system. As well, it reflects the budget constraint of the system; and this budget constraint provides the basis for the maximizing behavior of the individual and the firm.

Consequently, the overall output or income variable of Model B is relevant to both microeconomic and macroeconomic systems. This resulted in Model B, while having a macroeconomic character, yet being a microeconomic system in being based wholly on the behavior of the individual and the firm.

19.10 Concluding Remarks

We have in this book, through resolving an inconsistency in the orthodox classical system, Model A, arrived at a more general approach to price systems compared to the orthodox approach; and this was reflected in the new approach providing the basis to integrate microeconomic and macroeconomic systems, systems that are dichotomized in the literature.

This was illustrated in detail through Model B, our revised classical system, that reflects our new approach to price systems. However, this new approach to price systems goes beyond the specific Model B.

This is because we may use this approach to form more detailed and complex systems compared to Model B; and our analysis should be extended to cover such systems. There are also various other ways in which the work of this book should be extended.

Thus we should base the new systems in the book explicitly on the maximizing behavior of the individual and the firm; since while our systems are consistent with this behavior, we left this behavior implicit in our analysis.

This allowed us to focus on the main issue of the book which was our bringing into the new systems, an aspect to the behavior of individuals and firms that is missing from the orthodox systems. Finally, the stability properties and issues about the existence of solutions to the new systems should also be covered.

Index